PSYCURITY

Across the world, the rhetoric and violence of white supremacy is rising up. Yet, explanations for white supremacist attacks typically direct attention toward an unreasonable, paranoid state of mind, and away from the neocolonial security state that made them.

Offering a response to US expressions of white supremacy, Liebert reads paranoia as a dis-ease of coloniality by following its circulation within the ultimate place of reason, indeed a key arbitrator of it: Psychology. Through reflexivity, interviews, participant observation, scientific artefacts, and public art, this unique work seeks to argue for and experiment with unsettling the entwined coloniality of Psychology and the current political moment, joining with struggles for a world where it is not only white lives that matter. Tracing the spinning cogs and affective coils of the prodromal movement – a program of research that, capturing potential psychosis, illustrates the serpentine workings of a control society – Liebert argues that, within a context of *psycurity*, paranoia hides as reasonable suspicion, predicts the future, brands threatening bodies, and grows through fear, thereby seeping into the cracks of white supremacy, stabilizing it. Catching this argument as itself enacting psycurity, she then engages the more-than-human to search for paranoia's decolonizing, otherworldly potential; one that may revive the *psykhe* – breath – of psychologies too.

Calling for psychologies to leave Psychology's comfort zone and make space for imagination, this performative, interdisciplinary work will engage students, researchers, and activists from an array of disciplines who wish to examine a critical and creative response to present-day racism and fascism.

Rachel Jane Liebert, from Aotearoa New Zealand, has a Psychology Lectureship at the University of East London and a Psychology PhD from the City University of New York. Seeking to breach the genocidal legacies of her settler and intellectual ancestry, she collaborates with decolonizing and feminist scholarship, art, and activism.

Concepts for Critical Psychology: Disciplinary Boundaries Re-thought
Series editor: Ian Parker

Developments inside psychology that question the history of the discipline and the way it functions in society have led many psychologists to look outside the discipline for new ideas. This series draws on cutting edge critiques from just outside psychology in order to complement and question critical arguments emerging inside. The authors provide new perspectives on subjectivity from disciplinary debates and cultural phenomena adjacent to traditional studies of the individual.

The books in the series are useful for advanced level undergraduate and postgraduate students, researchers and lecturers in psychology and other related disciplines such as cultural studies, geography, literary theory, philosophy, psychotherapy, social work and sociology.

Most recently published titles:

Psycurity
Colonialism, Paranoia, and the War on Imagination
Rachel Jane Liebert

Beyond Care
Boundaries to Science, Health and Subjectivity in Capitalism
Owen Dempsey

Queer Politics in India
Towards Sexual Subaltern Subjects
Shraddha Chatterjee

PSYCURITY

Colonialism, Paranoia, and the War on Imagination

Rachel Jane Liebert

LONDON AND NEW YORK

First published 2019
by Routledge
2 Park Square, Milton Park, Abingdon, Oxon OX14 4RN

and by Routledge
711 Third Avenue, New York, NY 10017

Routledge is an imprint of the Taylor & Francis Group, an informa business

© 2019 Rachel Jane Liebert

The right of Rachel Jane Liebert to be identified as author of this work has been asserted by her in accordance with sections 77 and 78 of the Copyright, Designs and Patents Act 1988.

All rights reserved. No part of this book may be reprinted or reproduced or utilised in any form or by any electronic, mechanical, or other means, now known or hereafter invented, including photocopying and recording, or in any information storage or retrieval system, without permission in writing from the publishers.

Trademark notice: Product or corporate names may be trademarks or registered trademarks, and are used only for identification and explanation without intent to infringe.

British Library Cataloguing-in-Publication Data
A catalogue record for this book is available from the British Library

Library of Congress Cataloging-in-Publication Data
A catalog record for this title has been requested

ISBN: 978-1-138-70179-3 (hbk)
ISBN: 978-1-138-70180-9 (pbk)
ISBN: 978-1-315-20387-4 (ebk)

Typeset in Bembo
by Swales & Willis Ltd, Exeter, Devon, UK

CONTENTS

Acknowledgements   *vii*
Series editor's preface   *ix*

1   Terrain   1
    Blood 1
    Borders 8
    Book 11

2   Machine   17
    Terror 17
    Reason 21
    Prodrome 23
    Smoke 28
    'America' 31
    Serpent 35

3   Cogs   40
    Nets 42
    Borderguards 50
    Custody 61
    Search 66
    Fuel 73

vi Contents

4 Coils   77

  Legacy   78
    Desire to Know   78
    Ignorance   79
    Fear of 'regressing'   80
    Paranoia   83
  Psycurity   85
    Hiding   86
    Predicting   87
    Branding   88
    Growing   90
  Supremacy   91

5 Roots   96

  Wound   97
  Cliff   99
  Coatlicue   101
  Borderland   104
  Ecology   107
  Beside-the-mind   111

6 Compost   115

  Space-making   116
  Re-turning   119
    Ingesting/excreting: mystery   120
    Tunneling: ritual   122
    Burrowing: pausing   124
  Magical ideation   127

7 Serpent   130

  Otherworldly correspondence   131
  War on imagination   134
  Weaponless   137

References   143
Index   154

ACKNOWLEDGEMENTS

Four years in the making, this book-creature has witnessed a transformative time – painful, joyous, loopy, fearful, resolute. I am indebted to the following who kept us tethered during this period. To Michelle Fine for your mentorship, and Sunil Bhatia, Cindi Katz, Linda Alcoff, and Patricia Clough, for your questions, guidance, and openness. To Colin Ashley, Michelle Billies, Ali Lara, Wen Liu, and Akemi Nishida, for the theory, writing, critique, radicality, and wine. To Holli McEntegart, for the magical ideations. And Oliva Holmes for the photography, and Wiremu Woodard for the advice. To the prodromal researchers for your generosity. And Arthur Zitrin for the connection, and Sarah Illingworth and Emily Andrews for Sandy Hook. To el Jardín Etnobotánico de Oaxaca, the people and the plants, for hosting us. And the Public Science Project and Authority Research Network, for incubating my more-than-human praxis. To Priya Chandrasekaran and Stephanie Davis, for your brilliant eyes and fierce hearts. To the New View Campaign, Icarus Project, Occupy Wall Street, OccupyCUNY, Free University, Watching Floyd, The Porn Project, Red Hook Rises, and Outsider Gallery London, for teaching me about mad, gender, racial, and educational justice. And the US, Nepali, Jordanian, and Chilean activists I met during the International Honors Program, especially Kierra Sims and Mabel Cobos, for unblocking me. To Leonore Tiefer for everything. And Nicola Gavey and Virginia Braun, for being such a solid ground. To Adeola Enigbokan, Kendra Brewster, Deshonay Dozier, Monique Guishard, Alexis Halkovic, Amber Hui, Dominque Nisperos, Fernando Quigua, Ola Rayska, Whitney Richards-Calathes, Sonia Sanchez, Puleng Segalo, Kate Sheese, and Jen Tang, for bringing *psykhe* to our studies. To Rebecca Fullan and Amanda Matles for thinking about white women against white supremacy. To students at the City University of New York, International Honors Program, and University of East London, for doing mystery, ritual, and pausing. To Ian Parker and Eleanor Reedy, for your patience and flexibility. To Fulbright, Bright Futures, American Association of University Women, City University of New York, Jane Douglas, Paul Wiggins, Chris and Di Liebert, Sam Liebert, and Mumtaz Noorani for helping with money. To Fir, for showing me science. And Mum, for showing me art. And Paul, for reminding me. To my ancestors, for keeping me questioning. And the whales (and their riders). And Pirongia, for holding me accountable. And finally, to Tehseen Noorani, for your brain, your play, and your magic. I remember clearly that day, in your Baltimore kitchen, when you asked me the etymology of paranoia and we found that it meant beside-the-mind, forever shifting the shape of this project. Thanks for putting up with me. Ehara taku toa i te toa takitahi, engari he toa takimano.

SERIES EDITOR'S PREFACE

This strange, passionate and compelling book raises a crucial question about how we read and write in and against psychology. Among the many innovative conceptual questions about the intimate links between the nature of colonialism and distress – how the one is normalised and the other is pathologised – the book raises a profoundly methodological one. Not only is the treatment of textual material addressed, challenged and reworked so as to transform our understanding of what is usually referred to as 'data' in standard psychological studies, but the way in which we read them is intensively reflected upon. The different kinds of material – written and visual – are examined and analysed, deeply analysed through the deliberate subjective position of the researcher and writer, Rachel Jane Liebert. She tracks the way discourse and affect are mobilised in what she calls the 'war on imagination', and she turns our capacity for imagination back on the phenomenon she names as 'psycurity' in such a way as to untangle the way it threads its way into all of our lives.

This book about 'psycurity', about the entanglement of psychology and psychiatry in the insidious and pervasive securitisation of modern life, is also necessarily about paranoia. How is it possible not to be tangled in the coils of paranoia when we are in the grip of the neo-colonial security state? And how is it possible to respond to that grip, and to find a way of disentangling ourselves from it, without engaging in a reading of its manifold forms that is itself paranoid? The courageous double-move that Liebert undertakes here is, first, to enter the domain of paranoia, to trace her way around its coils, and, second, to shift focus from the usual mode of reading 'data' in psychology, to move from a paranoiac to a 'reparative' reading. For, as becomes clear in the course of this book, psychology along with most other academic disciplines typically does engage in a 'paranoid' reading of phenomena, searching for underlying deep-hidden meanings and attempting to master them, showing that mastery in the quick-witted ability of the researcher to expose the text to their audience. The second move is to refuse to fight fire with fire and, instead of falling in line with psychology's usual claim to 'predict and control' the world, to trace a more creative, poetic, even surrealist path to a reparative response, a response which acknowledges how things mean what they mean and what our place in that meaning-making is.

Through seriously playful challenges to psychological method and forms of argumentation, *Psycurity: Colonialism, Paranoia, and the War on Imagination* works at the boundaries of subjectivity and objectivity to develop a postcolonial anti-racist practice in alliance with community activists. It is 'outwith' psychology in a peculiarly disturbing and inspiring way. On the one hand, this is about the imaginative response of an individual author, but in such a way as to ground that personal imaginative response in the public politically-accountable terrain of madness and protest. On the other hand, this is about the committed response to psycurity by one academic writer, but in such a way as to mobilise the responses of many others in an alliance of voices of protest. Each, and together, outwith the enclosed individual subject and outwith the objective academic scholar, Liebert takes us closer to revolution, with others instead of against them.

Ian Parker
University of Manchester

1
TERRAIN

Blood

I was raised in Aotearoa as a "New Zealander," first hearing the potential of otherwise from a Pacifica nurse treating me when, 14 years old, I awoke from an eight-hour coma. She was standing over my hospital bed, looking intensely at me, finally asking what ethnicity I was. Confused, I stammered, "New Zealander?" My ignorance answering her question: "You must be Pākehā."

On my father's side, my European ancestors first arrived in Aotearoa five generations ago, two decades after the signing of The Treaty of Waitangi and Te Tiriti of Waitangi – two supposedly identical yet significantly different documents, one in English one in Te Reo Māori, soliciting Māori acceptance of British occupation, of colonization. In 1863, my great-great-great-grandfather, Heinrich Pohlen of Germany, moved to the central region of the northern island – Tainui land – to fight in the war against Indigenous sovereignty. He joined the settler militia – a 100-man force known as the Forest Rangers – and soon after helped to lead a massacre against Rangiaowhia, a village designated as refuge for Māori elderly, women, and children during the war, and the main supplier of food for the anticolonial resistance. Eventually murdering 100 people, the Forest Rangers began by surrounding a house with seven people inside, opening fire, and then setting it alight. When an elderly man came outside with his arms raised in surrender, they shot him to death; everyone else stayed inside and died by burning. In exchange for this and other contributions to the war against Māori and Aotearoa, the settler government gave my great-great-great-grandfather 51 acres of stolen land. Three decades later he murdered his settler neighbor over a boundary dispute. Seen then as mad and dangerous, he was incarcerated in a lunatic asylum where he met his own death. Killed by the ownership he killed for. His body was, is buried in Rangiaowhia. Beholden to the land of the massacre that made him, that made my family, that made me.

On my mother's side, less is told but it is no less telling. My European ancestors were missionaries and wives of missionaries who arrived on the shores of the southern island of Aotearoa – Ngāi Tahu land. Having travelled from the United Kingdom through India, they played an explicit role in the destruction of Indigenous cosmologies, preparing the ground for the global spread of capitalism, colonization, white supremacy.

Skip forward to June 2017, and this past feels right beside me. In Charlottesville, Virginia, a group of white men march with tiki torches, yelling neo-Nazi slogans and violently attacking anti-racist and anti-fascist protestors, driving a car into a group of activists, killing someone. Chanting "white lives matter" and calling themselves 'Unite the Right,' the rally is in part a reaction to the increasing power of black, Indigenous, and immigrant resistance in the US. It is also part of a recent surge in the visibility of fascist rhetoric and movements in the global North more broadly – whether far-Right nationalism, securitized borders, militarized police, xenophobic policies, attacks on non-white bodies, swastikas in the street, or the victory of Donald Trump as 45th president of the US. An uprising that reveals colonization as an 'ongoing organizing force' (Rowe & Tuck, 2016). For fascism, as Robin Kelley (2000) writes following Aimé Césaire, is not an aberration so much as a "logical development of Western Civilization itself," a "blood relative of slavery and imperialism" (p. 20).

Indeed, contemporary white supremacy in the US is built on what Andrea Smith (2012) describes as three logics, or 'pillars': *slaveability*, which anchors capitalism; *genocide*, which anchors colonialism, and *orientalism*, which anchors war. The first, slaveability, depends on a racial hierarchy to justify the making of one as the property of another, taking the profits of labor. The second, genocide, depends on the disappearance of Indigenous peoples to justify the taking of native land and resources. The third, orientalism, depends on the marking of peoples or nations as both inferior and threatening to justify force in the name of protection. This last pillar presents itself most clearly these days in the 'war on terror,' intensified following 9/11 and manifesting as both the domestic surveillance of Muslim communities and the foreign occupation of majority-Muslim countries. Holding these histories and their current-day manifestations close, in this book I use the term *neocolonial security state* to refer to contemporary US conditions. In doing so

I hope to evoke the more commonly used 'neoliberal security state' with its intertwining of modern-day capitalism and terror (Katz, 2007), while at the time recognizing that neoliberalism emerged in response to twentieth-century anti-colonial movements that challenged the authority of capitalism (Harvey, 2007), and thus respecting the lead of decolonizing authors who argue that colonization and modernity cannot, must not, be disentangled (e.g., Mignolo, 2012; Sandoval, 2000) – as evoked in the term 'coloniality' (Maldonado-Torres, 2006).

Increasingly, as this neocolonial security state swells more and more around us, I try to return to my ancestors, to feel what they felt, to think what they thought. How could they have – knowingly or unknowingly – participated in genocide? There are many ways that others have entered and answered this question. For me, its power has remained in it being insoluble. Ultimately a mystery, my ancestors' violence obliges, urges me to endlessly watch for colonization's grip. This watching, they tell me, is part of my ability to respond, my present *response-ability* for their past actions.

It was Gloria Anzaldúa (1987) who first got me thinking about 'response-ability.' She writes of 'responsibility' as invoking not simply our contribution to something but our 'ability to respond' to it. And yet, while we live in cultural and political contexts saturated with calls for responsibility, these same worlds simultaneously 'shackle' us in ways that undermine this ability: "We do not engage fully. We do not make full use of our faculties. We abnegate." (p. 43). These words are quoted from *La Frontera: Borderlands*; this book, and Anzaldúa's writings in general, have been indescribably influential on the chapters that follow. As a Pākehā New Zealander, a descendent of European settlers, I was often not included in Anzaldúa's 'we,' whose theory explicitly emerged from her own flesh and lands – that of a Chicana philosopher and poet. Her guidance thus came to me not as an equation so much as a provocation. In this, my own book, I have tried to not simply uproot her work, placing it out of context and away from what animates it, to deaden it. But to plant it somewhere that shares Anzaldúa's spiritual and political commitments, to nourish its liveliness. That is, to ask for guidance as I try and create something that also challenges – in content and in form – a white supremacy built on not just human but more-than-human genocide.

In particular Anzaldúa's writing directed me to my own flesh as a source from which to do so. Frantz Fanon's (1952) *Black Skin, White Masks*, likewise argues and shows that "digging into the flesh" (p. 3) is a necessary tactic for expelling coloniality. While Fanon himself, a Martinican psychiatrist, was writing from and to an experience of blackness, it was digging into this that enabled him to also acutely theorize whiteness. For him, while a violently different experience to being black, white people are similarly both captive and core to coloniality; the way that whiteness is done, which does not necessarily require white skin, enables colonization to hold on. Thus, as with Anzaldúa, his words were a guide not for equating my experience with his own but for provoking it toward similar commitments. That is, to destroy whiteness as we know it, to decolonize.

With their shared attention to 'flesh,' Anzaldúa and Fanon challenged me to consider two kinds of response-ability within conditions of coloniality. The first: a listening to inspirited, embodied, worldly knowledges. Both scholars demonstrate that the colonial episteme can only be punctured with 'antennae' – a term they both use (see Anzaldúa, 2002; Fanon, 1952). The second: to consider the particular response-ability that comes with my white skin. Of course, white skin is not the same as whiteness,[1] and there is more to my body than my skin color – I am female, disabled, working class, immigrant. But don't let my words and intersectionality trick you. I move easily through the world, smothered in an inherited lube. In blood. My skin and veins are the skin and veins of my settler ancestors, of militia and missionary. Poisoned by coloniality (Césaire, 1955). If I am committed to decoloniality, I must include my body. What follows, then, is a response to the work of Anzaldúa, Fanon, and many others; an attempt to engage my flesh as a source for learning from and being in solidarity with an intellectual decolonizing movement that has been challenging white supremacy for over five hundred years.

I remember clearly the first time I *saw* white skin. It was only eight years ago. I was 29 years old and had just returned from South Africa where, staying with a black friend and colleague who grew up there, I had spent more time in solely black spaces than I had before. Back in New York City where I lived at the time, I was on the M-train when something caught my eye.[2] A white hand wrapped around a silver pole. *My* hand wrapped around a silver pole. I took it off and looked at it more closely, moving the muscles and bones of my fingers to push and pull at the skin. *It's white*. Before then, I *knew* I was white. I identified as white, regularly named whiteness, organized against white supremacy. But it was in this moment that I *saw* it. It was as though the light suddenly refracted off my skin and struck my retinas from a new angle. Or my retinas themselves had changed shape, receiving the light in a new way. I don't know what or how it happened, or barely even how to describe it. Only that the skin, my skin, now had a kind of *glow* to it. *It stood out to me*. Perhaps what Sara Ahmed (2007) would describe as 'surfaced.' I looked up and around the subway car and saw a similar skin encasing about half of the bodies around me. Not bodies, *white bodies*. Not people, *white people*. Reality shifted half an inch to the right. I felt faint, spinning.

I started to see white skin whenever it was there. Family, friends, students, colleagues, workers, partiers, strangers, mirrors. White people, so many white people. Sometimes I was completely surrounded and a feeling of slow terror would spread over my skin. *My white skin.* I was trapped. I had been trapped my whole life. And I was going to be trapped forever. On the white side of W.E.B. DuBois' (1903) veil, seeing the world through whiteness, whiteness as the world.[3] Closing in tight, I felt a desperate desire to tear it apart. To destroy. To escape. To breathe. Four years later and Eric Garner, a black man, was choked to death by police officers for selling cigarettes on the streets of New York City. His final words, "I can't breathe," became a rallying cry for black liberation and decolonizing activists around the US, UK, Western Europe, and South Africa. For "breathlessness," as Nelson Maldonado-Torres (2016) writes in his *Ten Theses* on de/coloniality,[4] "is a constant condition in the state of coloniality and perpetual war, but it increases in certain contexts" (p. 5). The difference between mine and Garner's experiences was and is stark and screaming. Fanon (1952) writes of white people sealed in whiteness, black people sealed in blackness; the former suffers through ignorance or anguish, the latter suffers through harassment or death. And yet to deracinate this murderous episteme, Fanon continues, we need to deracinate both.

Fanon concludes that the decolonizing potential of the body lies in its capacity to provoke questions. Having white skin surface after three decades of being white and half a decade of challenging whiteness, spun me out of a comfort I did not know I felt. Not to suddenly 'see,' arriving at a decisive state of 'woke-ness,' but to enter a perpetual mode of discomfort. Ever alert to the possibility of ignorance, complicity, injustice. And practicing how to turn this possibility into a driving force. This book is in many ways a product of this kind of uncomfortable praxis (Pillow, 2003); a reflexivity that does not simply purge the poison, leaving myself supposedly clean and others repeatedly cleaning up – whether with sympathy, interpretation, or reparation (Alcoff, 1991). But that creates questions that oblige my own response. Not with The Answer; with more questions. A spiraling *Q&Q*. Generating an energy that moves, struggles, unsettles. . . . *If my blood is poisoned, does it affect my reasoning? My vision? My respiration? Is my experience of breathlessness an appropriation of black and Indigenous struggles? A manifestation of my own white paranoia?*[5] *Of seeking to know, control, own? Am I simply evoking the spirit of my great-great-great-grandfather? Can I, should I expel him? Or does his presence make me alert, hold me accountable? Can I reclaim my flesh,* revive *my flesh,* the *flesh, without taking the air of others? Is air finite? Can I join forces with people to create fresh air? Or am I then 'saving,' bleaching, evoking the spirit of my missionary ancestors?. . .*

Scratching and piercing with my nails, stinging, my fleshy questions have spattered all over this book. Albeit tidied up with theories and quotes and citations. It was tempting to leave it that way, to make this first chapter quiet, rational, safe. Yet to do so would be to re-inscribe a colonial hierarchy of Knowledge, Knowing, Knower as detached, objective, universal. White. Peeling away the rational to expose the flesh, I instead have to, *get to* sense things. The skin is the largest sensory organ in the body, without a defensive layer it can touch and be touched. With this project I want to touch whiteness. To make it, to make me, flinch. Bleeding, vulnerable. Not in a way that welcomes me further along the path of heteropatriarchy and deeper into white supremacy, trading weakness for privilege. But in a way that screams, that fights, that follows the lead of the flesh. White blood cells dripping out of the colonial episteme. Slowly oozing, losing my defense from 'foreign' bodies. Exposed to Suzanne Césaire's "the strange, the marvellous, the fantastic" (as translated in Kelley, 1999). The beside. Strewn, stretched, my surface area increases, my sensory capacity increases. And so my ability to respond does too.

My response-ability as not a white person but a white woman hit me in 2015, with urgency, when I heard about my connection to another massacre by a young white man against people of color. Dylann Roof, an avowed white supremacist, shot nine black people to death during a church service in Charleston, South Carolina. At the time and in his online manifesto and FBI interview, he invoked white women as a reason for doing so: "You rape our women and you're taking over our country. You have to go"; "I have noticed a great disdain for race mixing White women within the white nationalists community, bordering on insanity it [*sic*]. These women are victims, they can be saved. Stop"; "Well I had to do it because somebody had to do something because, you know black people are killing white people every day on the streets, and they rape white women, 100 white women a day."

Roof's words were especially chilling because of their familiarity. One of the shackles that Anzaldúa (1987) names in her theorizing of response-ability is the circulation of 'protection' within heteropatriarchy and white supremacy. This joint circulation evidences how gender is shaped by coloniality and vice versa; the colonial Man did not include women. As Maria Lugones (2010) describes, while – unlike Indigenous and black women – white women were counted as fully human, this was dependent on a submission to white men. A relation that was violently established through 'witch-hunts' from the fifteenth century – executed first by the Church, then by the judiciary. Silvia Federici (2014) documents how it was the rollout of capital in western Europe that demanded this genocidal attack on women; the same capitalism that then demanded the colonial appropriation of land, resources, and bodies; the same colonization that then demanded the categorizations and hierarchies of white supremacy. Beaten into submission, since the end of the eighteenth century white women's bodies have been funneled by capitalist, colonialist, racist interests. And – as the 14-word slogan of the KKK attests[6] – this has often taken the form of protecting white women, controlling white wombs, maintaining white supremacy. Whether met with protest, tacit consent, active permission, or help – as the 52 percent of white women who voted in Donald Trump attests – we have become agents of the very violence that eradicated us.[7]

White women have a stake in, and a response-ability to, decolonization; feminism is hollow without a commitment to decolonization. And yet, as women of color have long pointed out, so often when done by white women it is seduced by the white heteropatriarchal power structure (Lorde, 1984), helping to pursue a universalizing, bleaching project. Colonizing (Mohanty, 2003). Much like Psychology. Federici (2014) further documents how it was people's capacities as healers, sorcerers, and performers of incantations and divinations that were persecuted during the witch-hunts; capacities that enacted the liveliness of the land, the non-linearity of time, and the relationality of our selves. In order to dominate it, capitalism required that the world be disenchanted and the abilities of the body to tune into this vitality – capacities embraced by witches – be exorcized. Alienated, this new Cartesian body was treated as a machine, as brute matter disconnected from knowing, wanting, feeling. Making its operations intelligible and controllable; constructing the prototypical individual with which Psychology is built and builds.

Sylvia Wynter (2003) locates this "de-supernaturalizing of our modes of being human" at the core of colonization (p. 264). For example, the people burned to death in Rangiaowhia by my great-great-great-grandfather and his militia comrades included the wife and two daughters of Kereopa Te Rau of the Ngati Rangiwewehi hapu of Te Arawa. Shortly thereafter, Te Rau became one of the original disciples and then leaders of Pai Marire – the first of a series of Māori spiritual movements committed to overthrowing settler dominance. Referred to as Hauhau – from 'the breath of God' – the movement became known for its violent tactics, terrifying settlers, launching a government campaign of repression against Māori spiritualities that culminated in the 1907 New Zealand Tohunga Suppression Act (TSA). Based on Britain's witch-hunting laws, the TSA criminalized tohunga – Indigenous healers rooted in relational ontologies that do not separate matter from spirit, mind from body, individual from world (Stewart-Harawira, 2005). Despite a liberal ruse of protecting Māori wellbeing, popular and judicial reports at the time explicitly show a desire to use the TSA to dismember the mobilizing, decolonizing capacities of tohunga (Voyce, 1989). And, as documented by Tūhoe psychologist Wiremu Woodard (2014), the TSA haunts contemporary mental health services in Aotearoa where Indigenous healers and healing systems continue to be "suffocated and subjugated" (p. 41; see also Taitimu, Read, & McIntosh, 2018). Violently declaring Man rationality as the only form of humanity, colonization braided the trajectories of women, Indigenous and black peoples, and the mad (Wynter, 2003). Current-day decoloniality demands a war against this war, a 'metaphysical revolt' in response to this 'metaphysical catastrophe' (Maldonado-Torres, 2016). Given that these incisions were and are reproduced through Science (including Psychology), Wynter (2003) suggests that combining Science with art may be one means to repair them, to resuscitate diverse modes of being human. Thus, driven by response-abilities emerging out of my settler, witchy, and intellectual ancestry, in this performative book I – a critical psychologist – draw on decolonizing scholarship, feminist science studies, and visual art to experiment with puncturing a twisted legacy of cosmological violence, reviving the *psykhe* – the breath[8] – of Psychology and therefore our response-ability within contemporary conditions of intensifying white supremacy, of breathlessness.

Borders

I take as my entry-point a desire moving through US media accounts of the Dylann Roof shooting – identifying and intervening on potential madness in young people in the hope of preventing US attack(er)s. Elsewhere, I have suggested that such pre-emptive psy[9] is a window to, an enactment of, a system of governance whose central function is modulating an affective tone of fear (Liebert, 2013a, 2013b, 2014). Following 9/11, this kind of governance was a tactic of "incalculable power" in the US, seeding a fascism that, Brian Massumi (2005) continues, "can only be fought on the same affective, ontogenetic ground on which it itself operates" (p. 47). Five decades earlier, Fanon (1952) is likewise noting how reason fails as an anti-colonial weapon because, contrary to how it presents itself, coloniality itself was and is unreason. These findings, which Fanon experienced as a traumatic betrayal of the intellect, loudly haunt the current day, where popular diagnosis laments the power of reason to persuade and explain fascism and white supremacy, often in turn labelling people as 'paranoid.' Indeed, post-9/11 conditions have been characterized by paranoia's omnipresence (Harper, 2008; Frosh, 2016) – including in critical inquiry (Sedgwick, 2003) and protest (Pignarre & Stengers, 2011).

Thus, in this book I use pre-emptive psy as a site for examining the circulation of paranoia within a neocolonial security state. However, while typically explained in terms of a 'surveillance society' awash with street cameras, email snooping, data storage, and government secrets (e.g., Frosh, 2016), this depiction of our Western paranoid milieu does not attend to the state stalking, attacking, and murdering of brown and black bodies simultaneously happening under the same regime. Paranoia is circulating within a post-9/11 context that explicitly incants suspicion for both the making of 'good' citizens and the quarantining, if not exterminating, of 'bad' – or potentially bad – ones (Puar & Rai, 2002). Keeping these politics of terror nearby obliges an analysis of paranoia that involves capital, race, and nation. My ear will therefore not only be to Massumi's (2005) affective, ontogenetic ground; I also attend to the ground of Aimee Carrillo Rowe and Eve Tuck's (2017) "grounded subject." Interrupting the "universalized subject of emotion, unmarked by geography or even social location – and 'innocent' of any complicity to settlement" (p. 6) otherwise lurking in studies of affect, the ground of this grounded subject is stolen Indigenous land.

As mentioned above, the project of Western modernity as a whole is inherently colonial and thus inherently colonizing (Mignolo, 2012). Rowe and Tuck (2017) therefore argue that settler colonialism demands urgent attention even in works that do not immediately appear to be concerned with Indigenous land. Indeed, to not do so is to perhaps participate in settler colonialism's tendency to 'cover its tracks' (Veracini, 2011) – an ignorance that capacitates white supremacy (Mills, 2007). Including, perhaps even especially, in Psychology. Drawing on Fanon, Maldonado-Torres (2016) posits that we should engage the psychological not as that to be medicated to fit into 'civilization' and 'progress,' but as a site of struggle around worldview and thus as that through which we could critically examine the workings of coloniality. In what follows then, I attempt to undertake a reading of paranoia as a *dis-ease* of white supremacy. This is not to suggest that paranoia requires white bodies, or that there are no other kinds of paranoia within white supremacy. It is to examine how whiteness – as emerging from and through coloniality (Rowe & Tuck, 2017; Smith, 2012) – may shape and move through paranoia in ways that animate a neocolonial security state. Following Ahmed (2007), I attend to whiteness in the hopes of bringing it to the surface, rather than allowing it to continue to be(come) given. Far from reification, by doing so I aim to protect us from its slipperiness, its worldliness, its comfort (for some).

However, decolonization is not a noun, something we pursue, but a verb, something we do (Tuck & Yang, 2012). As mentioned with Anzaldúa (1987) and Fanon (1952) above, attempts at decolonizing require attention to form as well as content. Hamid Dabashi (2015) writes how conditions of coloniality that have made one – the non-European – unable to think has also made the other – the European – locked into their worldview, unable to read a changing world. They thus recommend that we choose interlocutors who do not perpetuate the West as better thinkers than the rest, subverting what is considered legitimate theorizing in order to 'think otherwise,' to move toward 'an other logic.' This approach – what Walter Mignolo (2012), also guided by Anzaldúa (1987), calls *border thinking* – is said to invite a dialogue that, with practice, may open us to readings that lie beside a colonial episteme. And so, in what follows, I put European descendants of Cartesian-critic Baruch Spinoza (e.g., Karen Barad, Gilles Deleuze, Brian Massumi, and Isabelle Stengers) into conversation with non-European insurgent scholars who theorize the de/coloniality of the psyche yet have been ignored by the bleached canon of Psychology (e.g., Gloria Anzaldúa, Aimé Césaire, Frantz Fanon, Chela Sandoval,[10] Trinh Minh-ha, and Sylvia Wynter). I do so with a conscious intention to not "integrate and stratify all others within Whiteness," enacting my own white paranoia (Sharma & Sharma, 2003, p. 14), but to 'read forward' in such a way as to rupture colonial boundaries (Dabashi, 2015). To fracture – not expand – the epistemological empire of Psychology. Inviting psychologists to be resuscitated by the vitality of knowledges that, in their very existence, have breached conditions of coloniality, 'delinking' and 'disobeying' violent narratives otherwise imposed in the name of civilization and progress (Mignolo & Vázquez, 2011).

Including that coloniality is the only way. For Rolando Vázquez, a 'decolonial method' approaches its objects of inquiry with three aims:

> 1) To show their genealogy in western modernity that allows us to transform the universal validity claims of western concepts and turn them into concepts historically situated; 2) To show their coloniality, that is how they have functioned to erase, silence, denigrate other ways of understanding and relating to the world; and finally 3) To build on this grounds the decolonial option, as a non-normative space, as a space open to the plurality of alternatives.
> *(Mignolo & Vázquez, 2013, n.p.)*

Crucially, in what follows I try to not only show the *making* of paranoia and the *coloniality* of paranoia, but also the *plurality* of paranoia, departing from the Eurocentric fiction of one universality, trying to enact "at once the unveiling of the wound and the possibility of healing" (Mignolo & Vázquez, 2013, n.p.). More specifically, I engage a response-ability to look for the decolonizing potential of paranoia too, indeed to do more than the 'paranoid reading' typically demanded by critical scholarship (Sedgwick, 2003). For given that capitalism, colonization, and white supremacy all shapeshift (see Pignarre & Stengers, 2011; Rowe & Tuck, 2017; and Alcoff, 2006, respectively), anti-capitalist, anti-colonial, and anti-racist commitments require an approach that is equally as nimble. Philippe Pignarre and Isabelle Stengers (2011) suggest that this means any radical praxis cannot be akin to psychiatry – "whose diagnosis fills up hundreds of pages in the DSM, but whose means of intervention are desperately monotonous: pills and therapy" (p. 106) – so much as a cautious, collective, and continuous practice of un/making. A testing out of responses offered from the cracks in-between. This book, then, is also experimenting with this kind of experimenting. Critical and creative, paranoid and reparative, human and more-than-human, scholarship and art, scientific and poetic, academic and activist; my border thinking is as much about method as it is about theory.

Above all, like the recent work of Sunil Bhatia (2017), Suntosh Pillay (2017), and Glen Adams and colleagues (2015), among others, I hope that the chapters to come advocate for contemporary critical psychology to learn from and join with decolonizing scholarship and activism. While antipsychiatry and psychiatric survivor scholarship and activism has been drawing on the language of decolonization for several decades, this has often been as a metaphor and thus itself risks undermining rather than contributing to these movements (Tuck & Yang, 2012; Miller, 2018). To be clear, while I am likewise suggesting that the trajectories of Indigenous and mad peoples are connected through the colonial project (relying as it did on opposing the 'rational' and the 'irrational'; Wynter, 2003), I am *not* suggesting that the experiences of the mad mirror those of the colonized. Instead, I believe that these connections give critical psychology an obligation and ability to respond to the human and more-than-human genocide carried out within conditions of coloniality. Similarly, throughout this book I have chosen terms to analyze pre-emptive psy and paranoia (such as 'borderguards' and 'reasonable suspicion') that carry other contexts with them (namely the 'war on terror' and domestic policing). I do so not to suggest that the experiences of the mad mirror those who are terrorized by US security forces, but to suggest that the dynamics under scrutiny in this project may reverberate through different social struggles – connected as they are within the neocolonial security state.

Book

This book, then, is a decolonizing, feminist experiment to map an un/settling circulation of paranoia – how it is done, what it does, what it could do – in order to work through a critical psychological response to contemporary conditions of white supremacy.

And so, in the following chapter, *Machine*, I open with an account of the June 2015 shooting by white supremacist Dylann Roof, tracing how media representations direct explanation for his violence toward his unreasonable state of mind and away from the neocolonial security state. Wanting instead to offer a reading of paranoia as a dis-ease of white supremacy, I propose an alternative, ostensibly reasonable, site of analysis: the US *prodromal movement* to identify and intervene on young people who may become psychotic. While struggling and contested this program of research, known as 'NAPLS,' accelerated in response to the Sandy Hook mass shooting in December 2012, which led to investments in "a Homeland Security approach to mental illness." Curious about the forcefulness of this movement, I draw on published material as well as my own participant observation to propose a resonance between the prodromal movement and capitalism, colonization, and the 'war on terror' – three anchors of US white supremacy that could be exposed if the reason of the prodromal movement is called into question. Mobilized to defend itself and 'America' by singling out potentially sick people, the prodromal movement offers a rich site to examine the workings of a control society – a *serpent* that beckons description in order to figure out what we are being made to serve and to look for new weapons.

In Chapter 3, *Cogs*, I begin this task by drawing on fieldnotes from my participation in a school presentation, a prodromal training, and an interview with a Research Clinical Coordinator who was part of NAPLS, to describe the cogs of the US prodromal movement. I document how *nets* of suspect descriptions, early warning signs, and screening questionnaires are cast to capture potential prodromes. Pulled by a direct line, these "funny little kids" are then interrogated, standardized, and educated by *borderguards* that assemble them as potential psychotics, as suspects. They are subsequently held in prodromal *custody* through the threat of psychosis, and *searched* by studies for those parts of their experiences, lives, or flesh that point toward this impending illness. These four cogs enable the prodrome – now a set of little pieces – to be distributed across North America and put back together as algorithms to predict psychosis. Thus, the prodromal movement feeds itself with its own risk factors, making its own fuel for continued data production. All stuck together with a common sense that is made from urgency, trust, and compassion, these cogs create a machine that builds a wall around the prodrome, defending against the possibility that people's experiences are Normal – an infernal alternative that threatens and mobilizes the movement.

Having outlined its cogs, in Chapter 4, *Coils* I refocus my gaze toward the affective flows of the prodrome machine, the contours of the serpent that characterizes control societies. Lubricating a kind of Science bent on conquest, I first trace these coils through a colonizing desire-to-know, proposing that when this desire collides with a white supremacy capacitated by ignorance, it entangles with a fear-of-regressing to make paranoia. Taking knowing to forbidden places, this paranoia makes the pillars of white supremacy wobble, suggesting that white supremacy creates the affective conditions for its own dis-ease. I then offer *psycurity* as an abstract machine that trafficks this unsettling potential and contemplate its action in relation to the prodrome machine. Psycurity directs a rationalizing, controlling, and othering desire-to-know entangled with a fear-of-regressing to the irrational, uncontrollable, and other within, to *hide* as reasonable suspicion, *predict* the future, and *brand* threatening bodies. All happening within a hyper-saturated solution of not only Sandy Hook but 9/11, these looping coils of paranoia also *grow* through fear. Together, these serpentine movements ultimately erase difference such that, within psycurity, paranoia seeps into, rather than exposes, any cracks in the pillars of white supremacy, thereby animating, not threatening, a neocolonial security state.

However, having caught scent of my own paranoia and thus complicity with psycurity, in Chapter 5, *Roots* I experiment with a reparative reading of these same coils. Etymologically joining *para* (beside) with *nous* (mind), paranoia historically denotes an experience *beside-the-mind*. In an attempt to follow these roots, I stage an encounter between the prodrome and Coatlicue – a Mesoamerican goddess of the serpent who inhabits borderland spaces. I challenge the bifurcation of nature that splits reality and imagination in the prodrome machine, that poisons it with a colonizing binary of Truth and Illusion. I wonder if the prodrome's imagination is a place of negative prehension, radiating possibilities and otherworldly correspondence. And I ask if this potential encounters a psycuritized milieu that twists it into paranoia – arguing that, if so, paranoia's contemporary omnipresence may evidence a kind of ontologic injustice, a detaining of imagination at the gates of psycurity. In the arms of Coatlicue, the prodrome points to the vitality and the milieu of paranoia, reclaiming it as a capacity, calling for modes of attunement and apprenticeship. I thus argue for Psychology to take on a more extreme kind of empiricism – no longer asking *what should we do about paranoia?* so much as *what* could *we do* with *it?*

In Chapter 6, *Compost*, I put this imaginative leap to the test. I take on an apprenticeship with paranoia via *Missed Connections* – a multimedia installation performed in New York City and Tamaki Makaurau Auckland that changed the experimental apparatus of Magical Ideation, a psychometric ancestor of scales to determine the prodrome. I put my experience of *Missed Connections* into proximity with the ingesting/excreting, tunneling, and burrowing practices of worms to theorize how we might re-turn paranoia's roots, breathing new life into it. In turn, I suggest that practices of mystery, ritual, and pausing offer to fertilize, structure, and sustain a space for otherworldly correspondence

14 Terrain

within suffocating conditions. Obliging a compromise on what we Know, one to think/feel/act, and an art of immanent attention, these three practices can be approached as a mode of *magical ideation*, inviting a praxis that is *of* the imagination, not *on* it. Both composting and enchanting psycurity, this experiment offers psychologies fresh modes of response-ability within a neocolonial security state, re-turning the roots of our praxis too.

Lastly, in Chapter 7, *Serpent*, I reflect on what has unfurled in the preceding chapters as I have inadvertently theorized and enacted *otherworldly correspondence*. Witnessing and welcoming an entangled relationship, a partnership, with my object of inquiry as it has morphed between paranoia, imagination, magic, and war, I have critiqued paranoia with paranoia, listened to imagination with imagination, learned magical ideation with magical ideation, and advocated to fight war with war. All of which is a response to the prodromal movement, a machine within a control society, a serpent. My spiraling process has been a serpent eating its own tail. Arguing that psycurity effectively works as a *war on imagination* that violently divides not only human and human, but human and more-than-human, I suggest that to combat this war psychologies need to leave Psychology's comfort zone and regress, to move backwards in order to move forwards. And that the open body of the prodrome may offer an extra-ordinary strategy for doing so. I thus end by proposing *magical ideation* as a methodology of the oppressed that – demanding both servitude to decolonizing movements and weaponless psychologies – may help revive the psykhe of our studies and our response-ability within times of intensifying white supremacy, of breathlessness.

The cracks of each chapter also contain an ink drawing as an experiment in more-than-human theorizing. I speak more about this process in *Serpent*, for now I leave and encourage you to experience and interpret them as they come, freed of reason.

While accountable to Indigenous peoples, to people of color, to mad peoples, to anti-racist and decolonizing activists, this book is written for psychologists. Stretching the episteme of Psychology, I hope at least that the following pages stretch our boundaries, our skin, increasing our surface area. Expanding our capacity to sense, to correspond with an-other world, to imagine. Widening our ability to respond to suffocating conditions that murder most, and trap all.

Notes

1 In the US, for example, settlers were initially distinguished from slaves through the terms 'Christian,' 'English,' and 'free' (Jordan, 1968). It was not until slavery was threatened in the late seventeenth century, that 'White' emerged as an identity. At this time, poor whites were encouraged to mobilize along color, not class,

lines, in order to disrupt a potential alliance with black people that could otherwise have overthrown the white elite (Alexander, 2010). This new racial category allowed white supremacy to emerge, and 'whiteness' to become a performance – a way of being – affiliated with power; one that was and is more easily performed by people with white skin, but nonetheless is not dependent on this.
2 A reviewer for this chapter pointed out to me that Frantz Fanon's (1952) account of becoming aware of his blackness also happened on a train. I had completely overlooked this co-incidence and felt so uncomfortable about its implications of appropriation that my immediate reaction was to just exclude my own account from this chapter. Its inclusion does not mean that I no longer feel uncomfortable, but that I decided to keep this discomfort close-by, reminding me that I cannot simply shed my skin.
3 Here, I seek to evoke W.E.B. Dubois' (1903) theorizing of the veil worn by African Americans within white supremacy, at once separating black and white people, trapping and oppressing black people, and allowing black people to see into and know white people, without being seen and known themselves. By referencing a kind of 'white veil' I am not suggesting that white people experience the same thing. I am naming the other side of the veil, one of privilege and ignorance, while at the same time adding a nod to heteropatriarchy.
4 Following Karen Barad (2007), I use the slash as a device to indicate not 'and/or' so much as 'both and.' In this case, 'de/coloniality' refers to *both* coloniality *and* decoloniality, thus indicating that the two cannot be separated.
5 Sanjay Sharma and Ashwani Sharma (2003) describe how the white body is "mobile, deterritorializing, flowing – able to convert and connect to anything, like an all-purpose adaptor – a universal cultural assimilator of difference" (p. 13). This mode is paranoid, driven by a form of "delusional jealousy" – "*The truth is out there and the Other has something that I don't!*" (p. 13, their emphasis) – that manifests in a "pathological compulsion to integrate and stratify all others within Whiteness," to domesticate or destroy that which otherwise threatens to be "unknowable, untranslatable, uncontrollable" (p. 14).
6 'KKK' is the shorthand for Ku Klux Klan – a US terrorist organization that first emerged in response to nineteenth-century efforts to end slavery and continues to operate in the name of white supremacy and white nationalism. Represented with a '14' in Roof's own logo, their 14-word slogan reads, "We must secure the existence of our people and a future for white children."
7 In this book I at times interrupt the text with a 'we' (or 'us,' or 'our'). The 'we' that is evoked varies depending on the context – here it is white women, other times it is people with settler ancestry, other times psychologists. I deliberately do this in a slippery and intermittent way in order to try and destabilize this 'we,' undermining its potential to violently erase diversity. This potential notwithstanding, I bring it into the text in an effort to respect Eve Tuck and Wayne Yang's (2012) call to avoid "moves to innocence" within commitments to decolonization. In addition, given that forgetting is a necessary step in colonization, and ignorance a tool, I hope to periodically poke at an uncomfortable, generative re-membering for those readers who share in a 'we' with me.
8 'Psykhe' is the etymological root of 'psyche,' interpreted interchangeably as meaning breath, soul, or animating force.
9 I use 'psy' to collectively refer to the intellectual and practical traditions of psychoanalysis, psychiatry, and psychology.
10 Chela Sandoval (2000) undertook a similar 'litmus test' about the possibility of this kind of encounter for decoloniality in her book, *Methodology of the Oppressed*.

DRAWING 1. "Sensing." Black ink on cochineal print, el Jardín Etnobotánico de Oaxaca. Rachel Jane Liebert, 2016.

2
MACHINE

Terror

On June 17, 2015, a 21-year-old white male sat in a black church during a Bible study session in Charleston, South Carolina. After an hour, the group stood in prayer and Dylann Roof removed a Glock pistol from his fanny pack and opened fire. Nine people died; five people survived – three of whom were deliberately left alive "to tell the story." That is, that Roof had attacked the church because of his hatred of black people.

The following day, the *New York Times* (*NYT*) published a piece led by Frances Robles entitled, 'Dylann Roof, Suspect in Charleston Shooting, Flew the Flags of White Power.' Over the course of the article, accounts of Roof's violent racism were increasingly interwoven with accounts of his oddity; the final words are a quote from a friend that "He does weird things all the time" (Robles, Horowitz, & Dewan, 2015). Two days later, another article in the *NYT* by Robles describes the discovery of Roof's website that "offers the first serious look at Mr Roof's thinking" including imagery depicting a respect for the Confederacy, slavery, and Nazism, and a 2500-word manifesto outlining his white supremacist commitments and reasons for the attack (Robles, 2015). Roof is described in the article as "an unemployed former landscaper said to have a *fixation* on race" and a "*lone-wolf* extremist" (my emphasis). Scattered throughout the article are subtleties such as these that wrap his racism in individual obsessions; his expressions of racism implicitly becoming evidence of his state of mind. A month later, federal charges are bought against Roof for a 'hate crime,' an illegal act "motivated in whole or in part by *an offender's bias*" (FBI, 2018, my emphasis), once more directing attention to personal prejudices.

At the same time as these charges are announced, Robles and a colleague publish a third article. 'Dylann Roof's past reveals trouble at home and school' mines Roof's life for reasons behind the attack. After observing that Roof had been "reading white supremacist websites and, in the months before the massacre, boasted of wanting to start a race war," the authors state the following:

> But *nothing* in the records, and *nothing* in his friends' memories, offer a clear explanation to the question haunting South Carolina and the nation: How did the silent young man with no record of violence in his past come to be accused of killing nine people who had gathered to pray?
>
> "When he opened up, you could tell something was wrong at home. He wasn't at peace," said Taliaferro Robinson-Heyward, who attended middle school with Mr. Roof. "It wasn't like he was a mean person, but you could tell he had a darkness to his life."
>
> (Robles & Stewart, 2015, my emphasis)

The article goes on to search for a "clear explanation" by entering Roof's "darkness," which soon became synonymous with him being the product of a "broken home"; one that had included "a car that cost $700 a month, a 3,000-square-foot, custom-built home in Earlwood and four other properties, including two homes in the Florida Keys." Evoking a tired tendency to blame mothers, Roof is said to have become "strange" after his mother left his father ("claiming" he was abusive), "smoking grass," a "loner," "too smart," "scrawny," "quiet," "emotionless," "dressed in black," "loitering," and carrying both semi-automatic rifle parts and Suboxone – a prescription drug prescribed for opiate addiction. All characteristics that made him suspiciously different from his family:

> Several former neighbors, none of whom wished to have their names used because they did not want to be associated with the case, said the same thing: The Roofs were as normal as normal could be.
>
> Yet a website that Mr. Roof created included photographs of him with patches from white-ruled African governments on his clothes and others of him waving the Confederate battle flag. He sported the number "88" on his clothes, which appeared to be a reference to the white supremacist code for "Heil Hitler."
>
> On that website, investigators say, he posted a 2500-word essay that complained bitterly about black crime, citing incidents described

on the website of the Council of Conservative Citizens, a white supremacist group. He also praised segregation, saying, "Integration has done nothing but bring Whites down to the level of brute animals."

"A lot of people feel children learn that, they are taught intolerance and discrimination," Ms. Devine said. "I don't feel that is something Joe Roof would have taught or tolerated. Someone had to teach him that. So where?"

(Robles & Stewart, 2015)

By birth good and innocent, Roof has been corrupted by something perplexing. He is the abnormal to his family's normal, indeed his community's normal; an individual with clear signs of madness – the only explanation for the unexplainable. Despite that the authors' questions as to the *why* of Roof's attack are posed adjacent to their descriptions of his white supremacist activity.

Immediately after the shooting Roof was picked up by the Federal Bureau of Investigation (FBI). As with all the other evidence, the video of their two-hour interaction records his racist and heteropatriarchal rationale: "Well I had to do it because somebody had to do something because, you know black people are killing white people every day on the streets, and they rape white women, 100 white women a day" (Sack & Binder, 2016). And yet the engines keep working to locate this as mental instability. The *NYT* report on the content of this interview, continues that, "Given that many mass killers do take their own lives, or are shot dead by the police, Mr. Roof's extensive interview offered a rare courtroom glimpse deep into *the mind* of someone accused of such a rampage" (my emphasis). Glimpsing deep into the culture, the country, of Roof is not even suggested. Indeed, so naturally innocent, Roof was even described by the reporters as freed of his handcuffs and given a Burger King hamburger during the interview.

By November 2016, Roof is facing 33 federal charges including from hate crime laws punishable by death. However, following six months of requests from Roof, a court-ordered psychiatric evaluation has just found him competent to represent himself in his trial. Now legally obliged to grant Roof permission to do so, both the judge and Roof's own lawyers advise him that this is "strategically unwise" (Sack, 2016). For, while Roof's present competence does not speak to his past state during the shooting, they are concerned about him now refusing to present evidence that he did so while mad. As Kevin Sack's (2016) piece in the *NYT* explains:

> Death penalty experts predicted that Mr. Roof's trial, a deeply somber matter in a city still recovering from the massacre, would now take on elements of farce and reveal less than some hoped about

the psychological origins of Mr. Roof's alleged rampage. By controlling his case, they said, Mr. Roof may decline to present evidence of his mental instability that his highly regarded defense team might have emphasized in both the guilt and penalty phases.

(Sack, 2016)

Continue reading, and Robert Dunham, the executive director of the Death Penalty Information Center, is quoted as saying, "And often with mentally ill defendants whose murders were a product of their mental illness, they will attempt to justify their conduct instead of presenting evidence that their mental illness makes them less culpable." Further, and to end the article, Dunham states that, "When an emotionally disturbed defendant is permitted to cross-examine those witnesses and ask questions that may be based on a *delusional view of reality*, it only makes things worse" (my emphasis).

Concerns about Roof's self-representation are effectively about his refusal to tell a certain story about the shooting, a story of mental illness. Instead, as noted elsewhere with concern in the article, allowing him to represent himself, "could provide Mr. Roof with an unobstructed forum for his white supremacist views." In doing so he is thought to perhaps be, as one investigative journalist describes, "intentionally hiding his mental state" (Duncan, 2016); there is no question that "his mental state" is *there*, lurking, suspiciously hiding itself; there is no accepting that his acts were *rational* within the context of US racism and coloniality. Instead, Roof is put forward as "a deeply disturbed delusionist" (Blinder & Sack, 2017); his irrationality explicitly and urgently evoked in ways that conceal the politicized nature of his killing.

Roof continued "*denying* any psychological incapacity," called no witnesses, presented no evidence, and ignored his court-appointed lawyers (Blinder & Sack, 2017, my emphasis). In January 2017 he was sentenced to death by a unanimous jury made up of nine white people and three black people. His family is quoted in the *NYT* as saying that, "we will struggle as long as we live to understand why he committed this horrible attack, which caused so much pain to so many good people" (Blinder & Sack, 2017). Having refused the court's offer of mental illness, the why of Roof's terror is invited to remain elusive. Indeed, even a month after the decision, the *NYT* publishes a piece entitled, 'Trial documents show Dylann Roof had mental disorders,' sharing the now unsealed contents of his court-ordered psychiatric evaluation (Sack, 2017).[1]

Once again, a mass shooting by a white man – even when explicitly done in the hopes of starting a race war – is reduced to an individual biography, to that which bred a mental illness. Locating attacks in wayward psyches, ignoring the cultures of whiteness, heteropatriarchy, and militarism that produce them. A dynamic intensified within post-9/11 US conditions whereby 'mass shootings' need to be differentiated from 'terrorism'; revealing Roof and other national attackers as politically motivated interferes with representations of Islam as the source of terror, as the enemy against which 'America' stands tall.[2] A pillar itself of white supremacy (Smith, 2012).

Reason[3]

The *NYT* (2016) published evidence online from the Roof trial, including footage of Roof entering and exiting the church before and after the shooting, a video of him being interviewed for two hours by the FBI after his arrest, and his 26-page journal, manifesto, and hand-gun application.[4] Roof's journal seems to be where he drafted his ideas, which were then consolidated in the manifesto. In the journal he describes the Trayvon Martin[5] case as "the event that truly awakened me" for not only was it "obvious that Zimmerman was in the right" but this event,

> . . . prompted me to type the words "Black on White Crime" into Google, and I was never the same since. The first website I came to was the Council of Conservative Citizens: there were pages upon pages of these brutal, disgusting black on white murders. I was in disbelief. At this moment I realized that something was very wrong. How could the news be blowing up this Trayvon Martin case while hundreds of these black on white murders got no airtime?
>
> *(Journal, p. 3)*

Following, there is a section headed, "Blacks," that contains racist rhetoric about biological, psychological, and social inferiority; rhetoric that reeks with colonialism. He goes on to also differentially denigrate "Jews," "white women," and "Hispanics," although he considers "East Asians" potential "allies of the White race" (p. 4). Psychology and homosexuality are also targeted – the former for inventing mental illnesses, the latter for not being seen as one.

Roof says that the problem with white people is that they are not "racially aware," that they need to "view everything that happens through a racial lens" (p. 6). "We are told to accept what is happening to us because of our ancestors wrongdoing. But it is all based on historical lies, exaggerations, and myths" (p. 7) – whether the intensity of violence against black people, the pervasiveness of slave-owning by white people, or that segregation was oppressive. The last he describes as established "to protect us from them," including that "it protected us from being bought down to their level" (p. 8); and later that reinstating slavery would allow white people to "take back" the US even if they are the "minority" (p. 12). In turn, he despises the emergence of the suburb post-integration as "it represents nothing but scared White people running. And that's what they are doing. Running because they are too weak, scared, and brainwashed to fight" (p. 9). From page 12 there is a section headed, "Race War" that begins, "I would love for there to be a race war."

The manifesto ends with a section entitled, "An Explanation," that he has "no choice": "We have no skinheads, no real KKK, not one doing anything but talking on the Internet. Well someone has to have the bravery to take it to the real world, and I guess that has to be me" (p. 5). His final paragraph reads:

> Unfortunately at the time of writing I am in a great hurry and some of my best thoughts, actually many of them have been left out and lost forever. But I believe enough great White minds are out there already.
> *(Manifesto, p. 5)*

On page 18 in his journal a lone faded sentence reads, "I am not fighting for what White people are, but what we have the potential to be." This is repeated on page 23. The first and last pages have his website address, "lastrhodesian.com"[6] and the back cover has what appears to be Roof's personalized logo, including "14," "88," and the swastika. All overt symbols of white supremacy.

Roof has gone out of his way to explain, without a doubt, that his killing was a political act. Indeed, to clearly articulate his racist reasoning. What surprised me, however, was that in doing so he draws on many of the same arguments that one might find in a critical race analysis – recognizing that, as opposed to black people, white people don't think about their race; that "blacks are viewed as lower beings by White people on a subconscious level" (journal, p. 6); that "modern history classes instill a subconscious white superiority complex in Whites and an inferiority complex in blacks" (manifesto, p. 2), that "White culture is world culture" (journal, p. 9); that whites really move to the suburbs "to escape n____s and other minorities" (journal, p. 10, my removal); the emphasis on one's blackness, but not one's whiteness, in historical accounts; the dominance of whiteness in Central and South American television (manifesto, p. 4); and that patriotism ignores everyday violence (manifesto, p. 4). However, according to Roof, the view means black people are "held to a lower standard" and therefore "able to get away with things" (journal, p. 6); the history classes are naming a tough truth; the culture means that white people don't know how to see and appreciate their culture; the escape to the suburbs means that there is no one left to fight for white people; the accounting is ignoring the "numerous, almost countless wonderful things Whites have done" (journal, p. 14); the dominance of whiteness in media shows a respect for whiteness; the ignorance of patriotism means an ignorance of the violence experienced by white people. Every observation opens to a racist truth; there is no reasoning Roof out of his reasoning.

This 'fixity' is part of the American Psychiatric Association's definition of paranoid delusion, a symptom of Psychotic Disorder. Yet, reducing Roof's ideas and actions to a paranoid state of mind is to ignore their colonial reason. In this book, rather than dismissing the role of paranoia as a disease of the mind, I attempt a reading of it as a dis-ease of white supremacy. In Chapter 4 I suggest that – as a *desire-to-know*, to be a "great White mind" entangled with a *fear-of-regressing*, of losing "what we have the potential to be," "being bought down to their level" – paranoia not only makes sense within a neo-colonial security state; it animates it. And to get there I trace its circulation through the ultimate place of reason, indeed the arbitrator of it: Psychology. I take as my entry-point a desire moving through the Roof-esque media – that is, US accounts of mass shootings by young white men – identifying and intervening on potential madness in order to prevent US attack(er)s.

Prodrome

My site of analysis is a transnational program of research to identify and intervene on young people who may become psychotic – an experience most associated with a diagnosis of Schizophrenia. Catalyzed in 2014 by another mass shooting by a young white male (Adam Lanza, as discussed in more detail below), this self-proclaimed 'movement' (see Candilis, 2003) is curled through with some familiar tropes. The following is written by three of its founding figures:

> The anxiety generated by the news of risk can also be a benefit insofar as it heightens vigilance. One feature of this research is the close monitoring of a patient's clinical state. An activity that is maximized if everyone becomes more watchful and knows what to watch for . . . Psychosis often arrives like Carl Sandburg's fog; that is, silently, on little cat feet. Its progressive losses and changes are easy to ignore, to explain away, to minimize. Appropriate attention and concern for what is transpiring too often is delayed until the situation spirals into a crisis requiring coercive intervention. First psychosis is major life crisis; anticipatory anxiety helps to attenuate the shock surrounding onset and its potential for chaos.
>
> (McGlashan, Miller, & Woods, 2001, p. 568)

Telling a young person that they are at risk of becoming psychotic is said to produce an "anticipatory anxiety" that may in turn prepare them for their approaching trauma. Published the same year as 9/11, this valuing of vigilance circulates with an imminent political climate – a 'banal terrorism' that encourages people to be highly attuned to potential threats, to be on the lookout for suspicious packages, suspicious people (Katz, 2007). While initial talk of identifying and intervening on pre-psychosis can be traced to the beginning of the twentieth century, it was at this time that there was a "strong resurgent interest" in this idea (Woods, Miller, McGlashan, 2001, p. 223). Indeed, one review of the literature notes that, between 1991 and 2011, "the explosion of interest in the literature has been remarkable," with a 100-fold increase over these two decades (Fusar-Poli et al., 2013, n.p.).

This contemporary research oscillates around the *prodrome* – a cluster of thoughts, feelings, and behaviors thought to be a forerunner to, and thus predictor of, psychosis. Introduced by Wilhelm Mayer-Gross in 1932, this term did not appear formally in the literature for another six decades (Fusar-Poli et al., 2014). Several years later and a handful of studies suggesting that the prodrome, if treated, could reduce the incidence of psychosis (e.g., Falloon, 1992), triggered the establishment in 1994 of the Personal Assessment and Crisis Evaluation (PACE) clinic in Melbourne, Australia, to systematically study this phase (Yung, 2003). Less than a decade later and prodromal research sites were active in 13 countries (Olsen & Rosenbaum, 2006), establishing a set of risk factors that claimed to distinguish a population of 'ultra high risk' (UHR)[7] youth 500 to 1500 times more likely to develop a psychotic disorder within two years when compared to the general population (Carpenter & van Os, 2011).

In the US, this movement has become dominated by the Prevention through Risk Identification, Management, and Education (PRIME) clinic in Connecticut, which developed the Structured Interview for Psychosis-Risk[8] Syndromes (SIPS; Miller et al., 2002) that soon became the most used instrument in Europe and North America to identify prodromes (Fusar-Poli et al., 2013). Designed to "define, diagnose, and measure change systematically in individuals who may be in a pre-psychotic state" (Miller, et al., 1999, p. 275), the SIPS evaluates five categories of Attenuated Psychotic Symptoms – 'unusual thought content,' 'suspiciousness,' 'grandiose ideas,' 'perceptual abnormalities,' and 'disorganized communication.' While originating to support a clinical trial on the ability of anti-psychotic drugs to prevent psychosis, the SIPS was foreseen to enable the collection of prospective data on the prodrome in response to a "growing acknowledgement" of the importance of this "paradigmatic shift" in psychosis research (p. 276). Its development occurred alongside an announcement by the National Institute of Mental

Health (NIMH)[9] that came to fund seven projects on the prodrome to improve diagnostic criteria, better characterize the prodromal stages, and refine risk prediction models. According to Jean Addington and colleagues (2007), these projects revealed several challenges to conducting prospective research on the prodrome, particularly with regard to sample size:

> Sample size is the principal obstacle to achieving rapid progress in prodromal research because, first, the annual incidence of new cases is presumed to be low (ie, no more than 1 case per 10 000 persons per year in the general population) and, second, these individuals are hard to find.
>
> *(n.p.)*

Thus, the initial seven projects joined with one other and formed a collaborative, multisite investigation known as the North American Prodrome Longitudinal Study (NAPLS). Also funded by the NIMH, the overall goal of NAPLS was and is to search for predictors of psychosis by generating the largest prodromal sample in history, thereby providing "statistical power and scientific scope that cannot be duplicated by any single study" (Addington et al., 2012, n.p.). Indeed, adding the SIPS and some of the most vocal advocates for prodromal research to this powerful 'n,' NAPLS has come to dominate the movement worldwide.

Drawing on the data of 370 prodromes, NAPLS' first study (NAPLS-1) generated a psychosis prediction algorithm (Addington et al., 2007) that – among other things – their second study (NAPLS-2) set out to replicate (Addington et al., 2012). To do so, they recruited 764 prodromes via "intensive community education efforts" including "academic detailing, grand rounds, educational talks, mailings, postings, websites and internet hits, and public service announcements" (n.p.), with each of the eight sites developing their own "extensive referral sources in their area, and routinely contact[ing] them personally" (n.p.). However, only 12 percent of this second sample became psychotic within two years, and as a whole they showed improvement in all symptom areas over their time in the study (Addington, et al., 2015) – suggesting that their sample may not have been prodromal after all. Nonetheless, in May 2015 NAPLS released the prodromal movement's first 'risk calculator' based on the NAPLS-1 algorithm to estimate the likelihood that a young person will become psychotic within two years; data for a third study (NAPLS-3) is being collected; a ninth site has been added to the project; and the results of a piloted large-scale early detection campaign are currently being analyzed. Rolled out across eight towns in Connecticut during 2015, this campaign was directed toward challenging 'stigma' and as such involved public education as well as professional outreach, detailing, and measures to 'hasten engagement' in mental health services (Srihari et al., 2014). While targeted at young people experiencing their first symptoms of psychosis, it utilized the SIPS and thus was also expected to pick up prodromes for referral to NAPLS.[10]

And so, the prodromal movement swells. And yet, since its inception, it has met with much critique, including within psychiatry itself. As summarized nearly two decades ago by its founding members cited above, these studies are "controversial because the existence of the disorder is not a fact but a probability" (McGlashan, Miller, & Woods, 2001, p. 564). At that time, this controversy emerged from concerns about high rates of 'false positives,'[11] minimal evidence of benefit from being diagnosed and treated as prodromal, adverse effects from antipsychotic drugs, potential harm from being told that one is at risk for psychosis, the potential for 'false negatives,'[12] and the ethics of doing such research with adolescents. One decade on, and these concerns were only heightened as prodromal researchers pushed for the inclusion of the prodrome as Attenuated Psychosis Syndrome (APS) in the fifth edition of the Diagnostic and Statistical Manuals of Mental Disorders (DSM-5; see Nelson, 2014).[13] Having this formal diagnosis was said to enable treatment of prodromal symptoms, reduction in untreated psychosis, studies of preventative treatments and interventions, access to healthcare, and development of treatment guidelines (Fusar-Poli et al., 2013; Carpenter, 2015). These proposed benefits were situated within a US context whereby health insurance companies will only cover treatment if people have a formal diagnosis, and pharmaceutical companies will only invest in research when they know there is a market for their products. Nonetheless, soon also challenged by over 15,000 individuals and over 50 professional organizations (including 15 additional divisions of the American Psychological Association) who signed an 'Open Letter to the DSM-5' that specifically called out APS for its questionable diagnostic validity, targeting of young people particularly vulnerable to the harms of antipsychotic drugs, and sparse empirical basis (Kamens, Elkins, & Robbins, 2017), the diagnosis was eventually moved at the last minute to Section Three of the DSM-5, re-categorizing it as an area requiring further study (APA, 2013).

The DSM debate shaped the conversation on the prodrome by changing how it is conceptualized[14] and, in particular, increasing the intensity with which the research is advocated. For example, a May 2015 special issue on the prodrome in the *Journal of Nervous and Mental Disease* repeatedly describes the "pervasive" nature (e.g., Dickerson, 2015) and "global burden" (e.g., Whiteford et al., 2015) of Schizophrenia that, combined with the lack of effective treatment for psychosis, gives "the bottom line" for early intervention or prevention (Dickerson, 2015). A piece by Thomas McGlashan (2015) – helping to establish the PRIME clinic and first author of the extract with which I opened this section – ends with a note that, "as long as we humans survive and thrive, the potential for psychosis will remain with us and be expressed among us," such that "prevention through early detection and intervention will always be required to attenuate the full-blown expression of this devastating disorder" (p. 354). And another founding figure, Patrick McGorry (2015) – helping to establish the PACE clinic and receiving the 2010 Australian of the Year award for his contribution to youth mental health – calls for using the prodromal movement as a model for the "radical reform" of mental health services across the globe in order to "save lives, restore and safeguard futures, and strengthen the global economy" (p. 310), ending with a claim that, "this exciting new field promises human, economic, and public health benefits on a much larger scale than could have been envisioned in psychiatry even a decade ago" (p. 316).

Two years on, and all mental health services in England have taken up this call (Yung, 2017), while the US prodromal movement continues to be "accelerat[ing] rapidly" (Jones, 2017). However, while more than 1500 studies of the prodrome have been published in the past two decades, the research remains dubious. Indeed, while a meta-analysis of approximately 2500 people diagnosed as prodromal by a range of instruments suggested an average risk of becoming psychotic of 18 percent six months after being diagnosed, which increased to 22 percent after one year, 29 percent after two years, 32 percent after three years, and 36 percent after three or more years (Fusar-Poli et al., 2012), this varied substantially between studies with the more recent research in particular suggesting that people's risk of becoming psychotic in fact *declined* over time (Fusar-Poli et al., 2013). Moreover, a recent review by Jim van Os and Sinan Guloksuz (2017) suggests that the movement is "conceptually flawed," including questioning if psychosis is really the object under scrutiny. Let alone that the movement reverberates with decades of critique by activists and scholars against the potential for medical models of madness to cause not only individual but social harm by pathologizing experiences and lives that might otherwise illuminate or challenge an unjust status quo (e.g. Bayer, 1981; Conrad, 1975; Fanon, 1963; Szasz, 1960; Tiefer, 2006; Ussher, 1991).

The prodromal movement is thus a peculiar mix of struggling *and* accelerating; beckoning the observation by Tony Seddon (2010) that, as something malleable, dynamic, and contradictory, the risk of madness can only be made intelligible when viewed in its political context. This proviso seems especially relevant for the prodrome given that psychotic disorders themselves enact very particular historical moments (e.g., Blackman, 2001; Metzl 2009).

As alluded to above, the turbulent rise in the prodrome itself perhaps makes the most sense when considered in the context of the simultaneous rise in US politics of terror. Thus, in order to understand the ongoing commitment to capture the prodrome – despite the paucity of return after nearly two decades of investment – in the following section I foreground the background within which the prodromal movement moves.

Smoke[15]

> Two things really struck me. The first was Jessica Rekos' grave, which included an obvious love for whales; a black one had been covered somewhat with leaves and flowers, and she had two pendants hanging from a small post on the right hand side with other special charms. The second was all the American flags included in people's graves. At first I thought they were just for the children who had been shot, but then I looked around and realized about 90 percent of the sites had them, flapping in the wind. It was so quiet they sounded like a gentle, slightly frenetic, hum.

This is from my fieldnotes on October 20, 2013, after visiting six small graves at Saint Rose Cemetery on Cherry Street in Newtown, Connecticut. I was there just days before the demolition of nearby Sandy Hook Elementary School. Both my visit and the demolition were a response to a mass shooting by young white male Adam Lanza a year earlier, resulting in the deaths of his mother, six teachers, 20 students, and himself. Described on National Public Radio (2013) as, to schools like 9/11 was to airports, the Sandy Hook shooting triggered large-scale investment to identify and intervene on young people at-risk of madness, as exemplified in the preceding plea by surgeon, professor, and US talk-show celebrity Dr. Oz on the national *Piers Morgan Tonight Show* (2012) that, "We need a Homeland Security approach to mental illness."[16]

Dr. Oz's call also echoed through January 2013, when the Aspen Homeland Security Group's (AHSG) counsel on the Sandy Hook shooting with the US Secretary included a statement that "individuals with mental illness *who are properly treated* have no greater risk of gun violence than those without mental illness. It is those who the safety net has not caught that pose the greatest threat," and that while one in five children are affected by some mental health issue, it often takes eight to ten years for them to be "*properly* diagnosed" (Shalett, 2013, n.p., my emphasis). Drawing upon the work of the 9/11 Commission, the AHSG went on to advocate for the use of security measures, public education campaigns and "validators" (such as clergy members, celebrities, and grassroots organizations) to "broadcast . . . mental health indicators" as a means to protect society from potential violence (n.p.). Notably an emphasis in synch with the National Rifle Association (NRA) who emphatically argued in response to Lanza that the problem is not guns so much as "insane killers" and thus that we need more guns not less (LaPierre, 2012). Indeed, the NRA predicted a 25 percent increase in membership following the Sandy Hook shooting such that it was soon claiming nearly five million active members, making it one of the most powerful conservative forces in US governance.[17]

Shortly thereafter, the Obama administration called for a large-scale package of mental health reforms to identify and intervene on young people at-risk of madness. The Whitehouse allocated $60 million for youth mental health intervention services and $15 million for Mental Health First Aid—a public education campaign that teaches community members how to identify and intervene on "signs of mental illness" *before* "problems become crises" – including prodromes (National Council for Community Behavioral Healthcare, 2013). This investment also called for a "nationwide dialogue on mental health"; come October 2013, and an official 'community conversation' with over 400 people representing 'the public' was held in Washington DC. I was one of 40 people facilitating the day. Scaffolded with pop music, energetic hosts, and group aerobics, the day opened with a reference to the Sandy Hook shooting, followed by a series of clinical presentations and discussion questions. Divided into groups of ten, participants' subsequent conversations were scribed onto a laptop and entered into a centralized data system, undergoing a 'live data analysis' that was immediately fed back in the form of 'top' answers (those that came up the most) and one 'gem' (a direct quote thought to be especially powerful). When asked for "solutions to the mental health problem" for 12 to 17-year-olds, the top answer was, "To educate them and the adults around them about the signs and symptoms of mental health"; the gem was, "If you see something, say something" – the slogan for the US Department of Homeland Security's anti-terror campaign.

In March 2014, the President's 2015 budget newly requested $484 million for the Mental Health Block Grant – representing 1 percent of all state and federal spending on mental health care – to fund programs for early intervention in serious mental illness in the hope that these would be used to implement evidence-based treatment and prevention strategies nationwide. Meanwhile, two months later, US Vice President Joe Biden gave a speech at the annual convention of the American Psychiatric Association (APA) in New York City (NYC) calling on a full house of 15,000 psychiatrists to "Imagine the possibilities" – "Imagine with all those young people if we had . . . tools of early detection to prevent mental illness from taking over their life" (Biden, 2014, n.p.). Published by the *Psychiatric Times* Editors as an online video alongside a dramatic instrumental, Biden's words have an even greater cadence when one considers that the APA has a membership of over 36,000 psychiatrists globally; the convention itself is so large that it needs to be booked at least ten years in advance to obtain the necessary meeting space and sleeping rooms.

In March 2015, the 19th International Congress of the International Society for Psychological and Social Study of Psychosis (ISPS) in New York City also included a plenary event – a panel entitled 'From Social Exclusion to Social Inclusion,' described in the program as a "dialogue focusing on high risk and early intervention in psychosis." The second speaker was Robert Heinssen, a director from the NIMH, who opened his talk with a disclaimer that he was presenting his personal views not the US government's, and that he had no personal financial interests with any of the companies that he was about to reference. Heinssen spoke of a "horrendous tragedy" in December 2012 – when "a young man with serious mental illness, untreated"[18] shot his mother, six teachers, and 20 Sandy Hook elementary school students – creating a "shocking event" that "galvanized the interest" of the US government in early intervention. Indeed, while before the Sandy Hook shooting four States had "committed to early intervention," Heinssen projected that a further 25 would join suit by the end of 2015 – suggesting a seven-fold increase in national investment in just three years.

At that point not knowing who he was, I was noting how much "he seems like a politician – in a suit, no notes, center-staged, slick," scribbling observations as Heinssen went on to enthusiastically speak to us – an audience of approximately 1000 people identifying as clinicians, researchers and/or users or survivors of mental health services – about the Early Psychosis Intervention Network, otherwise known as EPINET. Describing itself online as a national network among treatment centers for subthreshold psychotic symptoms, EPINET was designed to "link clinical sites through common data elements, data sharing agreements, and a unified informatics approach for aggregating and analyzing pooled data," with the hope that systematic analyses of this data "will accelerate research into psychosis risk factors, biomarkers of psychosis risk and onset, and pre-emptive interventions" (Heinssen, 2015, n.p.). Heinssen spoke of desires to double EPINET's nodes of data collection from 60 to 120 by the end of 2016, inviting us into his problem of "How to create a culture where early intervention becomes the norm in the United States?"

Come September 2017, and EPINET's success is attributed with the aforementioned "rapid acceleration" of the US prodromal movement (Jones, 2017, n.p.). Meanwhile, Heinssen soon emerged in my ethnography as one of the most influential figures more broadly. As the also abovementioned McGorry (2015) recently wrote:

> The role of Robert Heinssen in assembling and nurturing these national research collaborations and the leadership of the current NIMH director, Thomas Insel, have been absolutely crucial in ensuring that early intervention has been placed at the apex of the US mental health research agenda and furthermore is being realized. In a perverse yet positive twist, the recent shooting tragedies in the United States have focused attention and funding on the need to respond more effectively to emerging mental disorders in young people and have added moral force to the logic and evidence supporting early intervention and sustained care.
>
> *(p. 314)*

It is this "moral force" – added to the "logic and evidence" of the prodromal movement – that I am interested in, although it is the word *force* that especially catches my eye. During the evolution of the prodromal movement, the possibility of predicting and preventing psychosis has been routinely described as "alluring" (e.g., Candilis, 2003), "compelling" (e.g., McGlashan, Miller, & Woods, 2001), "remarkable" (e.g., Fusar-Poli et al., 2013), and "exciting" (e.g., McGorry, 2015). Yet, as pointed out by the NAPLS group, the "true positive prodromal incidence approximates the incidence of schizophrenia" – one person per every 10,000 people in the general population (Addington et al., 2007, n.p.).[19] Chasing one hundredth of 1 percent, why is this movement so moving?

'America'

As suggested in the vignettes above, the prodromal movement not only has the force of the Sandy Hook shooting behind it, but that of 'America'[20] – a white supremacist nation built on logics of slavery, genocide, and orientalism (Smith, 2012). Intensifying after 9/11, this neocolonial security state is curling in and around the prodromal movement. Six months after the attacks on the World Trade Center in New York City, past President George W. Bush launched a 'New Freedom Commission' on mental health. In his opening remarks at the University of New Mexico, Bush (2002) urged "everyday people" committed to "fighting evil" to become "soldiers in the armies of compassion" and "make America a welcoming place for people with disabilities," creating a "collective good . . . [that] will define the true value and character of our country." In turn, his Commission recommended the national roll-out of TeenScreen – a program of 'mental health check-ups' to identify and intervene on young people at risk of becoming mad.[21] Combined with Bush's words, this roll-out suggests that pre-emptive psy can help to facilitate a narrative of American exceptionalism; a familiar tactic in the 'war on terror' for depicting the US as the pinnacle of inclusivity and thus democratic civility, while diverting attention away from its complicity in violence happening both inside and outside its national borders. As described by Jasbir Puar (2007), the post-9/11 generation of "non-normative national subjects" was "paralleled and racially demarcated by a rise in the targeting of raced bodies for exclusion" (p. xii). America was not, is not a "welcoming place" for all bodies.

Within this context, 'risk' operates as a regulatory device for ascribing racialized embodiments of danger (Grewal, 2003). Elsewhere, I have commented on how the circulation of risk within post-9/11 psy practices generates a racialized splitting between "the good and the bad, the subject and the object, the mainstream and the abject, the choosing and the controlled, the consuming and the contained, the insured and the incarcerated" (Liebert, 2010, p. 337; Liebert 2013b). This potential for diagnoses and interventions to land differently on differently raced bodies – protecting one, policing the other – lurks particularly close to the prodromal movement given that African Americans are up to seven times more likely to be labeled Schizophrenic (Metzl, 2009). Indeed statistics from Medicaid – a health insurance program for low-income families and children in foster-care in the US, nearly 60 percent of whom are black, Hispanic, or 'other' (Child Welfare, 2015; KFF, 2016) – suggest that children are disproportionately prescribed antipsychotics, with children in foster care prescribed three times as many (Rubin, et al., 2012). Moreover, a recent federal investigation into antipsychotic use across five US states expressed concerns that children as young as four years old were receiving too many drugs, at the wrong dose, for the wrong reason (Levinson, 2015).

This disproportion can be traced to and through fears of blackness in the US. The Schizophrenia diagnosis first emerged in Western Europe as 'dementia praecox' – used to identify and intervene on people deemed to have a biological incapacity for personal responsibility (Blackman, 2001). This construct traveled across the Atlantic to join with colonizing pretenses that black people had a biological incapacity for freedom; if people escaped slavery they were diagnosed with having a medical disorder – 'drapetomania' (Cartwright, 1851) – and treated with whipping, hard labor, and toe amputation (Metzl, 2009). Thus, while initially in the US Schizophrenia landed on white female docility, in the 1960s – a time of increasingly visible black resistance movements – it was used to incarcerate

African American activists said to be suffering from "the protest psychosis"; posited by Walter Bromberg and Franck Simon (1968) as a disease of hostility, aggression, and "delusional anti-whiteness." Schizophrenia, then, took over the task of pathologizing blackness, preventing revolt, protecting white supremacy.

This shift from white to black bodies also occurred during the deinstitutionalization of psychiatry – a process of dismantling asylums that involved more drugs and more prisons, both of which are increasingly provided by private companies in the US. Schizophrenia's newfound affinity for blackness thus also marked the beginnings of psychosis' circulation within industrial-complexes that advance "the strategic twinning of pain and profit – the hijacking of structural inequality for ideological and economic gain" (Fine, 2012, p. 3). Such proximity is particularly alarming in the context of the prodromal movement given that pre-emptive psy means that one's potential threat can never be falsified, deferred but not dispelled by its preventative interventions (Liebert, 2013a); a dynamic intensified with regard to psychosis given the dominance of biomedical discourses that construct it as a chronic illness. If people are potentially psychotic then they are not only supposedly identifiable and treatable but also incurable, creating an infinite market that beckons the continued interests and influence of medical and security industries – both of which, alongside the NRA, have enormous influence on US governance.

Indeed, since its beginnings prodromal research has received considerable financial support from drug companies. For example, the abovementioned PACE clinic, which launched the global movement, was initially funded by Astra Zeneca, Bristol-Meyer-Squibb, Eli Lilly, and Pfizer, and seven out the 11 members of the DSM-5 Psychotic Disorders Workgroup advocating for the abovementioned APS diagnosis had financial ties to the pharmaceutical industry. These members explicitly called for this diagnosis as a means to attract more drug company investment (e.g., Woods, Walsh, Saksa, & McGlashan, 2010), ignoring evidence that such collaborations produce research that is more likely to emphasize the benefits and downplay the risks of antipsychotic drugs (Moncrieff, 2008). The abovementioned piece by McGorry (2015) likewise includes the disclosure that he received "unrestricted grant funding from Janssen-Cilag, Astra Zeneca, Bristol-Meyer-Squibb, Eli Lilly, and Pfizer, and honoraria for consultancy and teaching from Janssen-Cilag, Eli Lilly, Pfizer, Astra Zeneca, Roche, and Lundbeck" (p. 316); notably the same piece that also ends with the claim that the prodromal movement promises "human, economic, and public health benefits on a much larger scale than could have been envisioned in psychiatry even a decade ago" (p. 316). McGorry's funded vision illustrates the movement's potential to be a biopolitical strategy that regulates the profitable capacities of life at a mass scale (see Clough & Willse, 2010).

In terms of security, one potent site for such mass investment is the education system. US schools and colleges have been increasingly adopting Threat Assessment (TA) practices that call on staff and faculty to watch for 'early warning signs' of potentially threatening students in the name of violence prevention and community safety. While originating in a collaboration between the US Secret Service and Department of Education following the 1999 Columbine High School shooting, TA was especially pushed for in the *Report to the President* following the 2007 Virginia Tech shooting by Seung-Hui Cho, which led to an incorporation of 'mental health issues' and spread to 80 percent of campuses and universities throughout the country (Randazzo & Cameron, 2012). Calling on teachers to report 'bizarre and unusual' behavior,[22] TA exemplifies a recent turn to psy profiling that is threatening to make schools what John Protevi (2009) describes as one of the "most securitized spaces" in contemporary US. Likewise for Benjamin Reiss (2010), the classroom is "in danger of becoming a barely acknowledged zone of quasi-psychiatric surveillance, risk assessment, and preventative intervention" (p. 27). Pointing out that the abovementioned *Report* was co-authored by the then US Attorney General Alberto Gonzales whose tenure included warrantless wiretapping and the authorization of torture, Reiss continues that this reads as a somewhat "more chilling document" when viewed in its post-9/11 context. That is, as something that suggests a "chain of links between the national security apparatus and campus screening of the mentally ill" (p. 37); one that was likely lubricated by the shooter being both brown and foreign.

As well as tapping into racism, the biomedical models of madness that move through these interventions allow for threat to be located in some 'fundamentally' unruly bodies, displacing the insecurity of security mechanisms, further shaping the image of an exceptional nation (Seddon, 2010; Rose, 2010) – as conjured in Bush's opening remarks above. The prodromal movement, then, is swollen with a capacity to protect America. By identifying and intervening on young people who may become psychotic, it threatens to enact an exceptionalism, racism, and pathologization that can allow the neocolonial security state to simultaneously depict itself as superior, eliminate threats to this depiction, and profit from this elimination. And, in contemporary conditions, a desire for this protection seems particularly close:

> I write this in the aftermath of the barbaric terrorist attacks in Paris—a city which, in so many ways, represents civility and the highest

achievements of civilization. These cowardly assaults are an example of incivility and self-righteousness carried to its most malignant extreme. Today, darkness may enshroud the City of Light; but if we face this evil with strength and resolve, in solidarity with the French people, the illumination of reason may yet prevail.

(Pies, 2015, p. 2)

This is the postscript of a commentary that came into my Inbox on December 3, 2015, from the *Psychiatric Times*.[23] It began with the author – a psychiatrist and editor-in-chief emeritus, Robert Pies – telling us of its original title: 'Campus Protests and the Dearth of Civility.' The protests Pies is referring to are those involving "racial inequality and the harassment of minorities on college campuses" (p. 1). Also known as Black Lives Matter, they are part of a nationwide social movement emerging from centuries of racism and resistance in the US. Despite his admission that "vigorous protest is warranted" (p. 1), Pies goes on to associate it with narcissism, a symptom of "incivility." One that can be carried to a "malignant extreme"; his postscript ultimately associates Black Lives Matter with "barbaric terrorist attacks." That the supposed incivility of blackness was used to rationalize the barbaric colonization and enslavement of African peoples, and that it is from this history that the need to explain to white America that black lives matter emerged, is ignored by Pies. Chilling opposites, his anti-racism protestors and Dylann Roof have some things in common. Both threaten to reveal the racism of America, both lure a psy gaze that keeps this racism hidden, that sustains US white supremacy. Pies' call for the "illumination of reason" reads as a slogan for coloniality, for Psychology.

Serpent

Curled through with capitalism, colonization, and the 'war on terror,' the ostensibly reasonable prodromal movement makes for a rich site of analysis regarding the workings of a neocolonial security state. Particularly given that it typifies what Gilles Deleuze (1992) calls a *control society*. According to Deleuze, moves to identify and control potentially sick people and subjects at-risk started from the early twentieth century and accelerated after WWII – a period petrified by growing anti-colonial, anti-capitalist possibilities. While previously disciplined in institutions, within this new system people became modulated through 'checkpoints' that detect and judge one's movements, feeding information on patterns up to higher levels, and affecting us according to established, yet changing, algorithms (Massumi, 2015). Now controlling people in ways that are "undulatory, in orbit, a continuous network" (p. 6), Deleuze (1992) thus writes of society as having moved from a mole to a *serpent*. In response, he suggests that we need to "describe" this serpentine system, figure out what we are being "made to serve," and "look for new weapons" (p. 4).

The remainder of this book takes up this imperative. However, demanding particularly minute interventions, control societies require attention to particularly minute detail. In turn, Philippe Pignarre and Isabelle Stengers (2011) recommend entering spaces such as research laboratories that will allow one to do so. Thus, in the next chapter I draw on fieldnotes from my participation in a school presentation, a SIPS training and an interview with a NAPLS Research Clinical Coordinator, to first describe the cogs of the US prodromal movement.

Notes

1 I am deliberately not including the diagnoses here for risk of them distracting from my argument, which is one of the ways in which these evaluations problematically shape the discourse on Roof's shooting.
2 During a press conference a week following Roof's shooting, an FBI director rejected a suggestion that Roof instead be charged with terrorism, telling reporters he didn't see the murders as a political act. Yet, according to US Code, "terrorism" includes any violent or dangerous act intended to intimidate or coerce a civilian population or influence government policy or conduct. It is not difficult to see how Roof's shooting could come under this, so long as it is found to be violating state or federal law. But the US criminal justice system is not about to eat itself, to reveal the white supremacy on and for which it was built (Alexander, 2010). Indeed, the Southern Policy Law Center suggests that there has been an ongoing ignorance of white supremacist terrorism at the federal level, with the government more concerned about Islamic terror. This is despite that, of the 85 violent extremist activities resulting in death since 9/11, nearly three times as many were 'far-right wing' compared to 'radical Islamist' (US Government Accountability Office, 2017).
3 This section contains extracts from Roof's writings that are explicitly, violently racist. My decision to include them here has not been an easy one and is by no means resolved. Quite simply, in reproducing them I reproduce them. And, arguably, as a white person my doing so is particularly problematic. While the content of them reveals nothing that has not long been identified in critical race studies, my hope is that the analysis I bring to bear contributes something novel and helpful toward anti-racist work.
4 I accessed this material in full during December 2016, however one year later Roof's journal and manifesto appeared to be restricted to one-page only. Both were full of spelling and grammatical errors yet for readability I have decided not to mark them all with a '[*sic*]'.
5 On September 26, 2012, Trayvon Martin, a 17-year-old black boy, was shot to death in his father's fiancée's gated community in Sanford, Florida, by neighborhood watchman, George Zimmerman. Supposedly mistaking Martin's bag of skittles for a gun, Zimmerman claimed self-defence and was eventually acquitted, intensifying black resistance movements against police brutality.

6 This name is a reference to the white minority of what is now Zimbabwe, where white people enlisted white supremacists to fight against black people.
7 Now also called 'clinical high risk,' or 'CHR.'
8 Originally the 'P' stood for 'Prodromal' but in 2014 there was a decision in the movement to change it to 'Psychosis-Risk.'
9 Entitled 'Prevention and Early Intervention in Psychotic Disorders', NIMH (1999) invited "applications to study the early symptomatic manifestations of psychoses in the prodromal phase" because of the "highly disabling" nature of psychosis as exacerbated by delays in people receiving anti-psychotic treatment (n.p.).
10 Personal communication, April 2015.
11 'False positives' refers to those young people who are incorrectly deemed to be prodromal.
12 'False negatives' refers to those young people who are incorrectly not deemed to be prodromal.
13 This new category was previously called the "psychosis risk syndrome." However, the name change was an attempt to highlight current symptoms as the focus for treatment, rather than the risk that the symptoms might pose for future psychotic disorders (Fusar-Poli et al., 2013).
14 For example, it led to a shift away from conceptualizing the prodrome as an at-risk state. Instead, the popular metaphor being used is one of 'chest pain' – that is, that the prodrome is a sign that *something* is already up, which *could* be psychosis or something else. Any intervention can therefore be considered *secondary* prevention: the primary goal is to evaluate and intervene on the present symptoms and their present causes, the secondary goal is to prevent what may otherwise have followed. For William Carpenter (2015) this difference erases concerns about false positives that have continued to haunt the movement.
15 This section draws on fieldnotes that I collected from several sites between 2013 and 2015: a two-day visit to Newtown, Connecticut, where I documented what I could see, hear, and feel in relation to the December 2012 shooting by Adam Lanza, and participant observation as a community facilitator in the Obama administration's Nationwide Dialogue on Mental Health in response to this shooting, and an attendee at annual meeting of the International Society for Psychology Study of Psychosis where key people in the prodromal movement were giving plenary addresses. All occasions were initially documented with handwritten shorthand and photography, before being typed up and fleshed out in my research journal with as many quotes as possible. Unless otherwise noted, all extracts are from these fieldnotes.
16 Notably given as an interruption to the interviewer's point about gun control, Dr. Oz argued that "guns we can debate over and I'll let the politicians do that" before going on to complain that, unlike heart surgeons, psychiatrists' "hands are bound" as "so many rules govern what they're allowed to do [that] it makes it almost impossible for them to provide broad scale support."
17 On December 14, 2017, now-president Donald Trump invited NRA president Wayne LaPierre to an event commemorating the anniversary of the Sandy Hook shooting.
18 Adam Lanza wasn't "untreated," but this adjective often accompanies accounts of his shooting – a stickiness that draws attention to the context in which these accounts circulate.
19 A figure one hundred times *less* than the rate typically used (yet never referenced) in popular accounts of Schizophrenia.

20 I use 'America' as a trope that is drawn upon in US nationalist discourse post-9/11; one that, among other things, erases the non-US parts of the Americas.
21 While suddenly closed down in 2012, TeenScreen was quickly implemented in primary care and high school settings, with over 2000 active screening sites in 26 states across the US and elsewhere including Australia, Brazil, India, and New Zealand. The program's breadth was considered particularly controversial because it was fully funded by the pharmaceutical industry, suggesting it was effectively a large-scale marketing campaign.
22 This was a phrase in an all-faculty email that I received from the Threat Assessment team when I was teaching at a public university on the East Coast of the US; the email also signed off with the slogan of the US Department of Homeland Security's anti-terror campaign, 'If you see something, say something.'
23 The *Psychiatric Times* is a publication owned by UBM Medica to offer news, special reports, and clinical content related to psychiatry to psychiatrists and other mental health professionals. It has a monthly print circulation of approximately 40,000, and monthly online viewings of approximately 400,000.

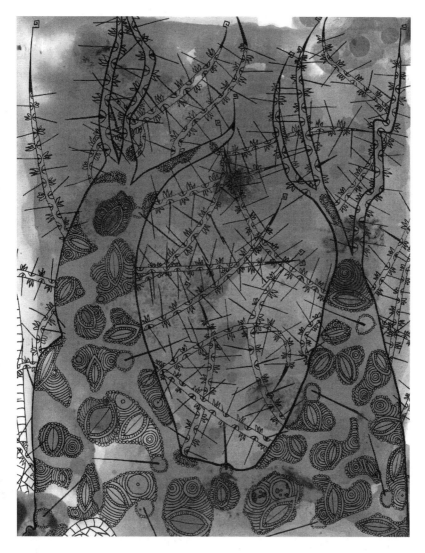

DRAWING 2. "Smoking." Black ink on cochineal print, el Jardín Etnobotánico de Oaxaca. Rachel Jane Liebert, 2016.

3
COGS

RCC: So this is where it gets complicated because we do a SIPS, okay? So maybe I do 80 SIPS a year, okay? But not all 80 people are gonna be prodromal. Some are already gonna be psychotic, some are gonna be non-prodromal, and some are gonna be prodromal. So I have to do that many SIPS in order to get 24 prodromes who will agree to be in the study. You know what I mean?

Me: Yeah that's the kind of math I was doing in my head but I–

RCC: Yeah it's a lot. You know it's a lot. And then again remember NAPLS isn't our only study so, you know? I'm now dividing up the people who are prodromal into the different studies that we have. So it, it's ah, it's complicated [chuckles]. It's very complicated.

Me: It sure is. And it's just– it's a lot of work. And so is that about how many SIPS you would do a year – about 80?

RCC: Yeah every year is different. This year– I can tell you where I'm at this year but–

[Turns toward wall; 2-second silence]

RCC: You know I have years when there's 69, years when there's, you know 78. You know it can be different.

Me: Is that a chart on your wall?

RCC: [Still turned toward wall] It is, it is. That's my motivator, keeps me going you know. I try to do better than I did last year you know.

Me: [Chuckles] Yeah I love things like that. So what is that? The list of the years and then the–

RCC: [Still turned toward wall] Right. So I wasn't there all of those years–
         [8-second silence]
Me: Mmm.
         [17-second silence]
Me: [Whispers] I have to– [Scribble sounds followed by soft murmurs]
         [9-second silence]
Me: So you're looking up how many? Is this a–
         [6-second silence]
RCC: [Still turned toward wall] So I'm at 76. Oh no– [Quietly to self] I'm more than that.
         [9-second silence; RCC counting under breath]
RCC: [Still turned toward wall; counting getting louder] 84, 85–
Me: Wow.
RCC: [Still turned toward wall; counting back to normal volume] 86, 87, 88. [Turns back to face me] 88 so far this year.

(Interview)

    This exchange marks a distinctive intensity during my interview with a Research Clinical Coordinator (RCC) who was part of the North American Prodrome Longitudinal Study (NAPLS), as introduced in Chapter 2. It occurred after an hour of talking together in her small office – tucked away in the corner of a prodromal clinic. She was sitting behind her desk in front of a computer with a noticeboard on the wall to her right, I was sitting opposite with my notepad and digital recorder in front of me. Up until this point RCC had by and large been responding to my questions with the same tone and content (sometimes word for word) that I had by now encountered during two earlier events that she had facilitated. Yet, here her demeanor changed. Stuttering when she named the amount of prodromes needed to meet the required 'n' for the various studies undertaken at the clinic, she was all of a sudden turned away from me, completely engrossed by a piece of paper on her noticeboard. It felt increasingly awkward – as illustrated by my initially breaking the silence with an "Mmm" and then my (more desperate) faux writing of a 'To do' list – finally ending when she had triumphantly counted to 88, her total number of 'successful' Structured Interview for Psychosis-Risk Syndromes (SIPS) so far for the year.

    Having considered the prodrome's movement within a control society in the previous chapter, below I enter my awkward silence with RCC to describe, in minute detail, the cogs of the prodromal movement. In doing so I use Philippe Pignarre's and Isabelle Stengers' (2011) lens of *infernal alternatives* – those possibilities that must be routinely denounced in order to defend a Truth.

Activating knowledge production as a mode of defense, infernal alternatives thus become a force that mobilizes scientists. The previous chapter suggests that, with regard to the prodromal movement, the infernal alternative against which researchers defensively mobilize is the possibility that people's experiences are Normal.[1] Its critics are concerned that *if* people are Normal *then* they are wrongly diagnosed and treated, subjected to negative effects on their sense of selves, their bodies and their lives; prodromal researchers defend against this by pointing to the potential harm and impingement of rights for someone who is *really* pre-psychotic, ignoring the possibility that people might be Normal. Importantly, this infernal alternative not only threatens the legitimacy of the prodromal movement. As also suggested in the previous chapter, this program of research is smoldering with the violent and ongoing creation of 'America'; one that could otherwise be exposed if the reason of the prodromal movement is called into question.

Here, then, I shall attend specifically to the scientific operations that work to block the infernal alternative of Normality. In doing so I describe the cogs of a machine that effectively builds a wall around the prodrome, allowing the movement to make its own fuel for data production while preventing us from smelling its smoke. Unless otherwise noted, all extracts are from my fieldnotes.[2]

Nets

> "These are the kids who" you don't want to sit next to a window as they're "hypersensitive to sunlight," or that are "overwhelmed" by noise and chaos in the school hallway so you might want to let them leave class 30 seconds early as this will make a "world of difference" to their stress levels.
>
> "It's the girl who says 'my friends are just pretending to be my friends,'" and her friends and you can try and tell her that that's not true and "offer proof," to "use rational thought to change her," but this isn't going to work: she's "irrational." Instead you need to use distraction.
>
> "These are the kids who are hypersensitive" to light, noise, busyness, to whom colors seem brighter. Someone jumped in and made a joke about one of the colorful paintings in the office – that 'these' kids would not like that, and that they could use it as a test. Everyone laughed.
>
> "These are the kids who can't keep pop culture in check" – when vampires and werewolves were "all the rage" recently they "actually believed it" – they were afraid of what was in their backyards at night-time.

"These are the kids who" believe in "aliens," "UFOs," "any type of alternative philosophies out there."

"Remember, these are the kids who" perceive stress strongly and overreact, or get a "wooden" or "poker" face as they'd "rather not emote" than be wrong. Or who all of a sudden have a drop in personal hygiene and appearance. RCC listed off a few examples, including "not wearing make-up" – a clear telltale "sign of prodromal."

(School fieldnotes)

A week before the interview above, I had taken these fieldnotes down in rapid succession. I was sitting in the principal's office of a middle school – surrounded by dark varnished wood, leather chairs, framed paintings, vases of flowers, approximately two-dozen teachers, guidance counselors, and administrative staff, and an over-representation of khaki and pastel. We were around a large rectangular table, with packets of outreach handouts, small plates of nuts, and a basket of water bottles in the center. A projector screen was at one end and our facilitator – RCC (dressed in black and white) – was standing at the other, controlling the slides and speaking. She was giving one of her after-school presentations on the prodrome, having been invited after a staff member had heard about her doing the same at the local high school.

We were two thirds through RCC's one-hour time-slot, and up to the 29th slide, when she started to describe young people who fit the description of a prodrome. The speed and repetitive structure of her list ("These are the kids who...") accelerated an urgency already brewing in the space. RCC had opened by saying that their clinic "specializes in the prodrome," that it's really important to get "help as soon as possible" as "the sooner they are identified, the better the prognosis," and that they were "very pleased" with the outcomes of the hearings following the Sandy Hook shooting – "millions of dollars" had been allocated to the field of early intervention, so they "have the resources now to do this really right." Not even needing an introduction, the ghosts of Sandy Hook were called even closer by.

RCC had then proceeded with what I noted as an "onslaught of info" – "so many half-articulated ideas, peppered with a jargon that when really listened to simply don't make sense." Indeed, I increasingly had the impression that:

> a lot of people don't really understand what she is saying but are agreeing because they want to get it and also because they don't need to get it – the point is simply that RCC and her clinic are experts.
>
> *(School fieldnotes)*

This sense only grew as RCC picked up the pace of the school presentation, at one stage saying about the SIPS that "she 'won't go into detail' about the 'validity and reliability studies' – (everyone laughed) – but they're there if people want them, and that it is 'being used around the world.'" Now moving fast through the slides (often too fast for me to even take notes), RCC could throw in jargon and a professional – indeed, *global* – norm, dousing the space with authority and showing that she was now fully established as "really into her science/knowledgeable/an expert set apart from everyone else." Directly after the presentation I further noted how this style merged with a lingering

> air of concern in the room – this was clearly a really serious topic for people yet at the same time they had just been thrown so much information – it feels like they've just let it wash over them, no one seemed to be taking any notes.
>
> *(School fieldnotes)*

Thus, the collision of intensity and passivity both thickened the urgency mentioned above and produced an ooze of expertise. The titbits of advice scattered in the suspect descriptions with which I opened this section, for example, felt to me "like gold nuggets." With the specificity and simplicity of these interventions carrying them as particularly knowledgeable and grounded, RCC "really, really established people needing her." This was exemplified by the painting joke in the third description, which, far from the comic relief that one might assume, instead portrayed the sense of comfort that was in the room. RCC was coming across as a trustworthy figure who knew both the technicalities and the seriousness of the prodrome, and who could help.

This trust in part came from the authority of Science, which entered the space with RCC's prestigious university affiliation and explicitly showed itself on the fourth slide of the presentation:

> RCC started to say how they know that psychosis is not genetic because of adoption twin studies that show that it is "not 100 percent concordant in monozygotic twins," and that in order to "avoid the deterministic view of mental illness" they "emphasize lifestyle and environmental factors." The most common were "substances" and "stress." With regard to the former, she said that they don't just mean things that are "illicit" but also prescription, explaining that many young people are going through the mental health system "misdiagnosed" – they are prescribed amphetamines and these will "exacerbate pre-psychotic

symptoms." People nodded and murmured agreement and concern. Someone asked if trauma was also "a risk factor," and RCC said yes, that there were "eight risk factors in total" – including trauma, maternal illness in the 2nd trimester, and if someone's mother "cleared cat litter while pregnant."

(School fieldnotes)

Filled with jargon, this extract exemplifies the way that Science was routinely gestured toward throughout the presentation – not only drawn upon, but also gently critiqued. Nods to the "deterministic view of mental illness" and young people being "misdiagnosed" implied a knowledge of *and* reflection on the psychiatric field that further cultivated a sense of expertise and trustworthiness.[3] The ease with which RCC responded to the risk factor question with a list of specifics only bolstered this authority – one that has a particularly watchful eye on mothers, and that can detect a suspicious package as seemingly benign as cat litter.

And that surpassed the skill of all of us in the room. RCC "really emphasized that while as people working with young people many of us will recognize these behaviors, they are 'not just being an adolescent.'" "Playfully warning everyone that she was going to get onto her 'soapbox'," she spoke of how while, "as people who work with young people we are all dedicated to 'encouraging young people to embrace their differences to an extent,' this should not be taken too far" – giving two examples:

> The first was a young woman who had "safety pins in the palms of her hands for months" and "no one had sent her for a mental health assessment?!" – because she was a Goth so people just accepted this as part of her self-expression. People gave noises of horror (at the girl) and judgment (at the people who had 'let this continue'). The second was a young man with long blonde hair ("It was 18 inches, I know because I measured it"), who used a type of glue to put it into a Mohawk and then wasn't able to sleep and "no one sent him for a mental health assessment?!"

(School fieldnotes)

As well as pre-empting critiques that the prodromal movement is pathologizing Normality, these patient descriptions conjured the perils of naiveté and ignorance – inciting people to send suspected prodromes for a mental health assessment.

A duty summarized through a question at the bottom of the slide projected during these descriptions, "Is someone you know at risk?" Summoned with the same cadence as the US Department of Homeland Security's anti-terror campaign, 'If you see something, say something,' a bright pink flyer in our stack of otherwise white handouts, the final slide of the presentation, and RCC's closing remarks all urged people to call RCC's clinic if they suspect anything, anything at all – "'If you hear nothing else please hear this phone number,'" ". . . 'anytime you think that a kid's got something going on,'" "'I don't care how minor the symptom is – that's what this clinic specializes in – go with it,'" "'If you just get them to us, or us to them, then we can get them on to an appropriate course of treatment.'" And her final words for the day: "'Please don't hesitate to contact me.'"

The "symptoms" we were to be on the lookout for were listed on the same slide – above the aforementioned question and under a heading entitled "Early Warning Signs of Psychosis." Nowadays a taken-for-granted phrase, both "Warning" and "Signs" almost covertly evoke a threat lurking beneath the surface: "Psychosis." This threat could be further detected through a 12-questionnaire screening tool that RCC offered twice to email through to us, and which is also easily available online. Respectively, I noted that people were "very thankful" and "murmured gratefully" in response to these offers – the latter of which was accompanied by RCC's point that, "'We don't want these kids to fall through the cracks, we know we can help them.'"

A repeated trope within mental health, "falling through the cracks" simultaneously summons both the image of a safety net and a need to tighten security. RCC used it herself in our subsequent interview, when explaining how the Sandy Hook shooting gave the prodromal movement more "momentum":

> I think Sandy Hook was a tragedy absolutely, and I think unfortunately a little bit because of his mother and a little bit because of the system he fell through the cracks and that's very sad. And we don't want that we don't want people to fall through the cracks you know. And so you know word of mouth, psychoeducation campaigns, I think they're so so important.
>
> *(Interview)*

While said in the context of wanting "to be very cautious to draw the distinction" between the Sandy Hook shooting and psychosis (because "usually they ['schizophrenics'] are not that organized to pull off something like that"), here the possibility of this event warrants "psychoeducation campaigns" – further showing how much Adam Lanza was in the air during our own psychoeducational experience at the school. Indeed, people's gratitude at receiving the abovementioned questionnaire seemed to embody the anxious shadow cast by this potential threat. The outline of which included a familiar, yet still ominous, intervening shape: mothers. Both participants and RCC made references throughout the school presentation to parents' ignorance or "denial" as a problematic barrier to identifying and intervening on prodromes. As she said in our interview:

> And again I can't stress enough our toll free number because you know they don't have to get parent permission to call us because we're never gonna name the person, we're just gonna talk in generalities – "I'm working with this student, this is what I'm seeing, what do you think?"
>
> *(Interview)*

Wrapping their phone-line in a promise of no charge and no names, RCC emphasizes that it can be used to elude an otherwise interfering parent. As a figure that always felt close-by in the school presentation, RCC thus aligned the movement with the school-workers while outwitting a familial harboring of suspected prodromes:

> First, a young woman who was sitting at the table one day and felt a cold wave come over and said that it was the spirit of her grandmother and was not distressed about it. However, she started to sit back at the table in the hope that it would happen again and ended up spending more time doing that than her schoolwork, seeing her friends, etc. (The implication being that she was therefore potentially pre-psychotic). Second, a young man who was bought into the clinic by his parents who were really, really distraught at the dramatic change in him – "something's happened," "he's hit a wall" – while he used to be an athlete, out with his friends, etc., he now just sits in his room all the time. When he spoke to RCC he told her that, what his parents didn't know, was that his friends had started to "smoke pot and drink alcohol and it's too hard to say no." This "was not psychopathology but good judgment" – "without having talked to him we would never have known."
>
> *(School fieldnotes)*

Unlike their parents, RCC was able to 'see through' the supposedly Normal behavior of the young woman and the supposedly pathological behavior of the young man. By juxtaposing these two skills, the latter protects the former from critiques that pathologizing is their default mode. Further, RCC used these examples to explain that, "'We can't measure what's going on in people's brains, all we can do is look at behavior and make assumptions about it.'" An inability to measure brains was further depicted as "the hardest thing" that they have to tell people – simultaneously locating prodromal experiences in a disordered neurobiology, making a trustworthy nod to the limitations of the movement, and aligning the struggles and desires of the movement with the struggles and desires of the people affected.

Indeed, described by RCC in our interview as all about "educating people about the early warning signs" – "I go to schools, I go to mental health clinics, I'll go to, you know, community outreach, NAMI, you know, PTAs, whatever. Anybody who wants to learn about this it's my job to go out and do those presentations" – community presentations are said to be driven by community needs:

> They are so relieved to know there is a resource out there. And you know especially with school systems they really love us because we're free. And with the school system if they make a referral the Board of Ed is liable for the money for that. So we're free so they can utilize us without worry. And so the schools love us.
>
> *(Interview)*

Caught through mail-outs for a "FREE staff training program" (their emphasis) and word-of-mouth (as RCC described, these are the main ways "that we get them"), community presentations and their associated assessments and interventions are framed as a comforting, empathic social service offered to under-resourced schools. For her, the "love" that they receive in response, is testimony to a "pendulum shift" – while "years ago when I started doing community outreach people's reaction was 'You guys are just inventing some new mental illness so some drug company can develop the drug to treat it'" now "when I go out and do the presentations the pendulum has swung completely the other way. Now people are looking at me going, 'Why don't we know about this?!'" Locating these initial concerns within a generic US cultural "attitude" to "question everything," RCC simultaneously dismisses any wonderings that the prodromal movement may be disease-mongering[4] and replaces them with an account that people could "really see the, you know, concrete use that it has and the difference it can make."

The "it" being the accommodations that RCC suggests to schools for their prodromes, some of which "are so minor." This emphasis on the small size of (some) interventions was given to again lift up the low cost to the schools in terms of time and effort, as juxtaposed against the benefits for all:

Prodromal kids are what "we lovingly call FLK's (Funny Little Kids)" – "everyone knows that something is up but nothing diagnosed" – in the past had to "wait and see" – don't want to do this as affecting the brain, especially the executive functions, and their primary occupation is students so frontal lobe issues make learning difficult.

(Training fieldnotes)

And you know think about it: We send these kids to school everyday to learn but with this illness their frontal lobe's not working properly and that's their executive functioning, that's what you need to learn. So we're sending them to school without the tools they need to learn. And then we get surprised when they get bored or frustrated and act out?! It's a natural sequence of events you know – "I can't come here every day and fail constantly without having some sort of reaction to that."

(Interview)

Here, during the SIPS training, RCC casts a suspicion around even seemingly harmless kids – their "something" will eventually reveal itself, and meanwhile will silently assault their schooling. Prefaced with an explicit call in our interview for me to, "Think about it" and an explicit performance of RCC's ability to stand in prodromal shoes, this "natural sequence of events" drew once more on the authority of Science and compassion to wrap common sense around the prodromal movement which, in essence, is 'simply' about these not-so-funny little kids getting the specialized treatment they need.

And you know, now– after this many years of doing this you know, there are psychiatrists and school psychologists and people out in the community that– we have a very strong relationship now and they'll call us right away and say, "Look" you know "I've got this patient let's get him evaluated just to make sure we're not missing anything." So I think what has actually happened is people are getting better care – "Rather than just assuming I know what's wrong with you and making a treatment plan, I'm gonna get a second opinion by people who specialize in this, and you know really make sure."

(Interview)

Evoking both a trustworthiness and urgency, RCC summons "better care" as the ultimate driving force of the community presentations.

Yet, in doing so, she avoids another agenda. The distribution of the suspect descriptions, early warning signs, and screening questionnaire are also casting a different kind of net – as often and as far and as wide as possible. When asked in our interview if people usually do call "the number" after the presentations, RCC replied: "Absolutely. Absolutely. You know it resonates with them and they'll say, 'Listen I have a student, this is what I'm seeing'":

> So we do post ads on Craigslist about the clinic and the services. The phone calls from people who saw it on the Internet are less likely to actually come in for the SIPS. They no-show on me, okay? The people who learned about us from a presentation come in. So probably 75 percent of the people who heard about us from a presentation will come in for a SIPS. Whereas probably about 30 percent of the people who heard about us on the Internet will actually come in for a SIPS.
>
> *(Interview)*

Seeing something and saying something, the community presentations lead to phone calls lead to young people coming in for a SIPS assessment, to standing at the gate through which they need to pass in order to enter prodromal territory – a place of research, a place of quotas. In the following section I consider how this crossing away from Normal is patrolled.

Borderguards

3–4–5
1. Began/worsened in past year
2. Occurring in past month an average of 1/week
3. Distress/interference
4. Not better accounted for by another DSM diagnosis
5. Mentions insight

(Training fieldnotes)

I copied this list down off a whiteboard in a very small, very hot, very bare room in the basement of a psychiatric hospital where myself, a research assistant, one graduate student researcher, and five clinicians/researchers were participating in a one-day training to learn how to use the SIPS. We were cramped around a rectangular table – scattered four-inch ringbinders of training materials and half-consumed donuts, bagels, and coffees in the middle, and a projector, screen, and facilitator (RCC) at the far end from the doorway. Nearing the end of the day, RCC was revealing her "cheat-sheet" – the three ratings and five qualities that turn an experience into a prodromal "symptom" – telling us that "lots of clinicians put these on a card and keep them by their side." As suggested by both "symptoms" and "clinicians," throughout this training (and the school presentation above), RCC routinely wrapped the prodromal movement in a biomedicalized discourse. This was despite also routinely making explicit disclaimers that she "hates that the SIPS is called a 'diagnostic instrument' because the prodrome is not an official diagnosis – it's only in the Appendix of the DSM-5."

Nonetheless, "diagnose," "diagnosis," and "diagnosing" were consistently used to declare when one crossed into prodromal territory. Assessed by the SIPS, our training day demarcated this threatening space, located between Psychotic and Normal. The first, supposedly more stable, border was that which separated Psychotic and Prodromal, patrolled by whether or not someone has the "insight" that their experiences are not "real" (as discussed further in Chapter 5). However, RCC spent the majority of time on the other, more unstable, border – that between Prodromal and Normal. Protecting the movement from its infernal alternative, this border was more heavily patrolled with the four other borderguards: 'worsening' (began or intensified in the past year), 'frequency' (occurring an average of once a week over the past month), 'interference' (causes an emotional or behavioral response), and 'fidelity' (not accounted for by another DSM diagnosis).

To learn these ways of watching, a series of nine vignettes were projected onto the wall next to the "cheat sheet" above, with 15 more in our binder for further independent practice. We had to rate the presence of a 'positive symptom' of psychosis[5] and then combine this with worsening, frequency, interference, and fidelity in order to make a prodromal diagnosis. However, the vignettes were purposely created with "gaps" in people's experiences – RCC emphasized that, while "anyone can ask the first question," "the trick" for those of us who would soon be experts in the SIPS is knowing when and how "to follow-up" versus "when not to follow a symptom":

> Slide entitled, 'UNUSUAL THOUGHT CONTENT': "Lori stated that she has always enjoyed thinking about different kinds of ideas and beliefs. Beginning in January 2007 the time she spent engaged in this activity doubled. When asked how much of her day is spent thinking about these ideas and beliefs she stated about 55 percent of each day. She was unable to provide specific examples of her ideas and her thought process became more tangential and loose as the interviewer gently pushed her for details. She stated that her brain seems different and it is bothersome and worrisome."
>
> RCC: She is showing two symptoms but her belief that her brain is different is a higher rank symptom so use this to make the diagnosis. If "can't get it there" then go to the next one. We don't know how often she

is doing it. We need to know the content – "don't back off" even if she is becoming more tangential and loose. P1 = 3, diag. = yes.

Slide entitled, 'SUSPICIOUSNESS': "Peter stated that at least twice a week, beginning in September, he has the feeling that other people are thinking about him in a negative manner. He stated that he can tell by the way they stare at him and then quickly turn away. He also reported a vague feeling that he is being watched. This occurs about once a month but he stated that he knows this is not real."

RCC: He shows two symptoms. Being called is higher rank but not frequent enough so go with the second one and check the level of conviction by asking if he asks people and how he reacts to their answer – "did you ever find out if it was true or not?" "Don't spend a lot of time asking questions that aren't going to get you a diagnosis." P2 = 3, diag. = yes. If calling out sick then P2 = 4.

Slide entitled 'PERCEPTUAL ABNORMALITIES': "Nicole stated that she hears her name being called about three times per month. This experience has begun in the past year and she is uncertain what to make of it. She reported that when she hears her name being called she often turn to look or asks someone if they heard it too."

RCC: She showed a reality check, not a change in behavior, but it's not frequent so it's not diagnosable anyway. P4 = 3, diag. = no. In clinical practice, would call Nicole back in a month as "may have just got them early in the prodrome."

(Training fieldnotes)

Lori and Peter were both deemed prodromal – the former for their unusual thought content, the latter for their suspiciousness. Schooling us to "follow a symptom," to move on if we "can't get it there," to not "back off," to not "spend a lot of time asking questions that aren't going to get you a diagnosis" and to call people back in case we "just got them early in the prodrome," the evaluation-*cum*-interrogation seemed driven by a desire to know where the prodromal symptom was hiding, a certainty that it was there, somewhere. Even if this meant broadening the jurisdiction of the borderguards: we were told at one point "don't get stuck on 'distress,'" that "people may not be bothered but they might be 'intrigued,' 'curious,' 'captivated,' 'find it weird.'"

Repeatedly saying, "What do you know and what do you need to know?" the reverberation of this command evoked the sense of a "hunt" that I also took down in my fieldnotes. This sense was furthered in both the SIPS training and school presentation when repeatedly told to "remember that there is 'a lot of noise going on in their head at this time and they don't want people to figure that out,'" that "young people go on the Internet and look up the symptoms, so 'we have to get better at asking questions' in a 'softer manner' – the SIPS is 'really good at this' – 'otherwise they know what not to say.'" Framing "these" young people as guarded, cunning, and deceitful, this tip dusted distrust over the prodrome while adding to the seriousness and expertise of the prodromal movement.

This mood climaxed in the last part of the day when we were given a one-hour simulation video of 'Natalie' – a real-life patient re-enacted by one of RCC's Research Assistants – being "interviewed" by RCC with the SIPS. RCC left the room, instructing us to individually watch the video and work through our own copy of the SIPS in order to evaluate whether or not Natalie was prodromal. I transcribed the script by hand, and quote here from my fieldnotes at length given that it was the pinnacle of our training:

"P.1. UNUSUAL THOUGHT CONTENT/DELUSIONAL IDEAS: PERPLEXITY AND DELUSIONAL MOOD"

RCC: "Have you had the feeling that something odd is going on or that something is wrong that you can't explain?"
Natalie: No.
RCC: "Have you ever been confused at times whether something you have experienced is real or imaginary?"
Natalie: In class I start daydreaming and when I snap out of it I have to refocus. Sounds silly.
RCC: Takes a few minutes?
Natalie: Yeah I have to figure out that I'm in class.
RCC: Bothersome?
Natalie: Yeah I don't know what I've missed, and it affects my grades.
RCC: How low have they dropped?
Natalie: At first I got mostly Bs now I'm failing a few.
RCC: When did this start?
Natalie: Last semester.
RCC: Early? Late? Middle?
Natalie: October/November.
RCC: How often does it happen?
Natalie: Every day.
RCC: "Do familiar people or surroundings ever seem strange?"
Natalie: Just when I come out of the daydream.

RCC: What do you make of what just happened to you?
Natalie: It's just weird. I dunno.
RCC: "Does your experience of time seem to have changed?"
Natalie: No.
RCC: "Do you ever seem to live through events exactly as you have experienced them before?"
Natalie: Like déjà vu? Yes.
RCC: How often?
Natalie: I don't know if it's déjà vu but sometimes I will have a dream and it's like the dream actually happens.
RCC: What do you make of that?
Natalie: It's not like I'm predicting things but it seems like a weird coincidence.
RCC: Happened your whole life, or new?
Natalie: I can't recall having it that often before.
RCC: When did this start?
Natalie: Summer.
RCC: After high school? June?
Natalie: Yes.
RCC: How often on average?
Natalie: A few times a month, not every day.
RCC: Every week?
Natalie: Yes.

"P.1. UNUSUAL THOUGHT CONTENT/DELUSIONAL IDEAS: FIRST RANK SYMPTOMS"

RCC: "Have you ever felt that you are not in control of your own ideas or thoughts?"
Natalie: No.
RCC: "Do you ever feel as if somehow thoughts are put into your own head or taken away from you?"
Natalie: No.
RCC: "Do you ever feel as if your thoughts are being said out loud so that other people can hear them?"
Natalie: Sometimes.
RCC: Can you tell me more about that?
Natalie: I've been concerned that I've been thinking of something and will see the expression on someone's face and I'm worried, 'Did they hear that?' And I worry 'cos if it's not a nice thing and I thought I just thought it.

RCC:	What do you make of that?
Natalie:	It's just my imagination.
RCC:	Is it concerning to you?
Natalie:	In the moment, as I worry that they know what I think, but they don't bring it up, so.
RCC:	When did this start?
Natalie:	I had it then it went away. I started noticing it again after I graduated high school.
RCC:	Is it happening more often or bothering you more?
Natalie:	No.
RCC:	How often does it happen?
Natalie:	Twice a month.
RCC:	"Do you ever think that people might be able to read your mind?"
Natalie:	Sometimes I think, 'Did I say something out loud?' but I don't think that they can read my mind.
RCC:	"Do you ever think that you can read other people's minds?"
Natalie:	No.
RCC:	"Do you ever feel the radio or TV is communicating directly to you?"
Natalie:	No.

"P.1. UNUSUAL THOUGHT CONTENT/DELUSIONAL IDEAS: OVERVALUED BELIEFS"

RCC:	"Do you have strong feelings or beliefs that are very important to you, about such things as religion, philosophy or politics?"
Natalie:	No.
RCC:	"Do you daydream a lot or find yourself preoccupied with stories, fantasies, or ideas?"
Natalie:	It's kind of embarrassing.
RCC:	That's okay, it's just us girls.
Natalie:	I got into Harry Potter and find myself fantasizing that I'm in them.
RCC:	In the books? The story?
Natalie:	Yes, I get lost in it.
RCC:	When did this start?
Natalie:	Summer.
RCC:	Before college?
Natalie:	Yes.
RCC:	Is that distressing?

Natalie: I like being there and spend a lot of time wishing I was but it's bothering my boyfriend.
RCC: Tell me more.
Natalie: He is making comments that I will just zone out and daydream.
RCC: Is this interfering with your ability to maintain a relationship?
Natalie: Yes.
RCC: So it's impacting you socially?
Natalie: Yes.
RCC: How often does it happen?
Natalie: Daily.
RCC: "Do you know what it means to be superstitious? Are you superstitious?"
Natalie: I believe in things like Friday the 13th.
RCC: Do you do anything differently because of this?
Natalie: Not really.
RCC: Does it bother you? Impact your behavior?
Natalie: No.
RCC: "Do other people tell you that your ideas or beliefs are unusual or bizarre?"
Natalie: Just the Harry Potter stuff.
RCC: Anyone else besides your boyfriend?
Natalie: I started to tell my friend but I don't talk about it anymore.
RCC: Do any of your friends read them?
Natalie: Yes but it doesn't seem like it's as important to them as it is to me.
RCC: Do you take it a step further?
Natalie: Yes.
RCC: What's your conclusion?
Natalie: Obviously it's not real but it's confusing, distracting.
RCC: "Do you ever feel you can predict the future?"
Natalie: Just when I dream, it can come true at least once a week.

"P.4. PERCEPTUAL ABNORMALITIES/HALLUCINATIONS: PERCEPTUAL DISTORTIONS, ILLUSIONS, HALLUCINATIONS"

RCC: "Do you ever feel that your mind is playing tricks on you?"
Natalie: All the time.
RCC: Tell me about that.
Natalie: At night when I'm driving I'll think that a mailbox or garbage can is a person and I'll do a double take.
RCC: So you're driving along and you'll see a mailbox?

Natalie:	And I'll think that it's a person and I'll be like, "It's a person." It's not only when I'm driving at night.
RCC:	Can be during the day?
Natalie:	In my dorm I'll see something and my dorm-mate isn't there and we don't have a pet, so.
RCC:	So it happens when you're in your dorm?
Natalie:	That's when it happens the most.
RCC:	How often? How many times if you averaged it out in the past month?
Natalie:	A dozen.
RCC:	Do you remember when this began? Was it before college?
Natalie:	The driving thing did, not often, just a couple of times, but the stuff in the dorm room is just since college.
RCC:	So it's getting worse?
Natalie:	Definitely.
RCC:	Does it bother you?
Natalie:	It freaks me out, I worry that it's haunted.
RCC:	Is it?
Natalie:	I don't know, sometimes I want my dorm-mate to stay home.
RCC:	What about driving – do you avoid it?
Natalie:	Yes, especially at night.

"P.4. PERCEPTUAL ABNORMALITIES/HALLUCINATIONS: AUDITORY DISTORTIONS, ILLUSIONS, HALLUCINATIONS"

RCC:	"Do you ever feel that your ears are playing tricks on you?"
Natalie:	No.
RCC:	"Have you been feeling more sensitive to sounds?"
Natalie:	No but I'll hear sounds outside my dorm room and will go and check.
RCC:	Is anyone there?
Natalie:	Sometimes. But sometimes there hasn't been so I'm like, "It's haunted," but then I'm like "No, that's silly."
RCC:	When you say "that's silly" is that because you know it's not real?
Natalie:	Yes.
RCC:	What does it sound like?
Natalie:	Like someone's there – footsteps, door closing – it's like someone went into their dorm room, it's not a big deal.
RCC:	You said you tend to hear more in the evening. Do you ever feel more nervous in the evening?
Natalie:	No, well only if I'm in the streets outside the dorm.

"P.4. PERCEPTUAL ABNORMALITIES/HALLUCINATIONS: VISUAL DISTORTIONS, ILLUSIONS, HALLUCINATIONS"

RCC: "Do you ever feel your eyes are playing tricks on you?"
Natalie: Just with the mailboxes.
RCC: "Do you ever seem to feel more sensitive to light or do things that you see ever appear different in color, brightness, or dullness; or have they changed in some other way?"
Natalie: No.
RCC: "Have you ever seen unusual things like flashes, flames, vague figures or shadows out of the corner of your eye?"
Natalie: Just the shadow thing in the dorm.
RCC: And the seeing didn't happen before college?
Natalie: No.
RCC: How often – as often as once a week?
Natalie: Yes.
RCC: In the last month has it been this often?
Natalie: Yes.
RCC: "Do you ever think you see people, animals, or things, but then realize they may not really be there?"
Natalie: Yes, and it's the mailbox or garbage can.
RCC: "Do you ever see things that others can't see or don't seem to see?"
Natalie: No.

(Training fieldnotes)

These extracts from my fieldnotes show the exchanges between RCC and Natalie that resulted in her being diagnosed as prodromal. 'P1' (Unusual thought content/Delusional ideas) because according to RCC her daydreaming "certainly reached the level of psychopathology and certainly changed her behavior," showed a "confusion between what's imaginary and reality," and "impacted her grades"; and 'P4' (Perceptual abnormalities/ Hallucinations) because she saw shadows in her dorm once per week, missees garbage cans and mailboxes as people, and does not want to be alone so has her boyfriend or roommate stay home ("even though she questions if it is haunted, she is distressed and changing her behavior"). By the time we were at 'first rank symptoms' I was noting that, "This questioning is so intense?!" – a feeling created by the speed with which they were being delivered ("we're all flicking through the binders at the same pace as RCC is on the video = fast – the sound of her pages turning is stark and disruptive and eerie") combined with the structured, closed-ended nature of the interview, requiring potential prodromes to give a definite affirmative or negative response. Only one of which is Normal.

Notably, *not* the response that 'we' were looking for. Come the section on 'overvalued beliefs' and RCC's 'successful' question about Natalie's daydreaming, "So it's impacting you socially?" and I am taking notes furiously that, "Everyone is taking notes furiously – there's a palpable sense of 'BINGO!' – it's like RCC is digging for gold with increasing skill and speed." Yet, far from unearthing prodromal experiences, by the end of the session it felt as if the SIPS was creating them. Bullied into predetermined binaries, they had little space to go – the structured nature of this interview standardized not just the questions, but the answers too.

A similar dynamic was also moving through RCC's talk about 'false positives.' The following extracts are from the school presentation and SIPS training, respectively:

> The main statistic that RCC wanted to draw people's attention to was that after 24 months nearly 70 percent of people who had been diagnosed as prodromal by the SIPS and not received any intervention had converted to schizophrenic psychosis, but also that at the clinic 100 percent of people who had not been diagnosed did not go on to convert. So, "If it's going to err it's going to err in the direction of false positive not false negative."
>
> *(School fieldnotes)*

> There are lots of different types of psychosis. One shortcoming of the SIPS is that it does not "split the hairs between affective and schizophrenic psychosis, but if it's going to err it will be towards false positive."
>
> *(Training fieldnotes)*

Especially given how central false positives are to critiques that the prodromal movement is pathologizing Normal, I was struck by how quickly this erring toward wrongly diagnosing people was glossed over. In fact, explicitly drawing our attention to it in the former and preceding it with a "but" in the latter, it was presented and received in both these settings as preferable.

This effect is testimony to the common sense that was steadily being established and grown throughout both the school presentation and the SIPS training that receiving the prodromal diagnosis is a good thing. When a participant asked in the SIPS training "In your years of practice, what's the most important thing?" RCC instantly replied with, "The psychoeducation piece is the most helpful, that initial evaluation." In our interview she elaborated on this:

60 Cogs

> As I said through my own experience – I don't have data to give you, this is just anecdotal – through my experience, the psychoeducation that occurs during the evaluation process, I see the difference that makes in my young patients and their parents. It's incredible. Because they have no clue – they think they're the only ones out there struggling with this, they have no idea how prevalent it is. And once you start to explain it to them and they see that other people experience this and that other people have been effectively treated, it really normalizes it for them. And it reduces their stress. And we've talked about this illness being a stress vulnerability illness. So anything that we can do to help them manage their stress is a positive thing.
>
> *(Interview)*

While careful to expertly differentiate data and anecdotes, telling "patients and their parents" during the SIPS that other people are prodromal *and* "that they have been effectively treated" is made central to the efficacy of the movement. Indeed, helping to "manage the stress" of this "stress vulnerability illness," this explanation is an intervention in and of itself. A slippage between evaluation and psychoeducation that further suggests people are prodromal by default.

Suspicious until proven otherwise, they pass through the gate and into the clinic:

> The SIPS is all about, 'Are they at risk or not at risk?' Now, because we're a research clinic, if they don't meet criteria for a prodromal– one of the risk syndromes, we can't work with them because we are mandated by our IRB.[6] That's the population that we work with so those people who don't meet a risk syndrome we have to refer elsewhere okay? Then the people who meet a risk syndrome, then we consent them to a study, if they want to be, okay?
>
> *(Interview)*

The prodromal movement casts suspect descriptions, early warning signs, and screening questionnaires within a fear-full context of under-resourced schools, problematic mothers, and potential shootings. Pulled by a direct line, potential prodromes are interrogated, standardized, and educated – assembling them as perhaps psychotic, as suspects. Blocking their infernal alternative, these operations allow prodromal researchers to make the "nice 'n'" both desired and required by the prodromal movement. Now with the fuel of prodromal bodies, in the following section I describe what happens inside prodromal territory.

Custody

RCC: One of the things that I love in particular about working for our clinic director – because research can be a tricky field, okay – and one of the things that I love about working with our clinic director is in the 17 years I've been here never once have I ever seen him put the research above what's best for the patient. He always makes his decision on "What's best for this person sitting in front of me?" And if it isn't the research he just pulls the plug and does what he needs to do to treat them. And I love that about him and about the work we do here at the clinic. Never ever do we put the research first.

Me: Yeah I wanted to talk about that actually. What is the line, or what's the difference between research and treatment? Because this is ultimately a field of research isn't it, technically?

RCC: Technically it is because if you look in the DSM-5 there isn't a diagnosis code for the prodrome it's only in the Appendix okay? So therefore it has to be considered research. But under that bigger umbrella of research we provide treatment. And we have options, and we explain those to the patient, "You can do this, you can do that, you can do this." And I think what's very important about our clinic is we offer that free SIPS assessment whether or not you wanna have treatment with us. There's no condition that you have to take treatment from us. We're gonna do that– we're gonna give you the results, make our treatment recommendations, you can go back to your own doctor and do it. So there's no coercion, it's totally volunta– 100 percent voluntary.

(Interview)

This declaration of RCC's "love" for her clinic director's approach came out of the blue during our interview. Colliding with the preceding affect of our conversation, it stood out as speaking to *something*, as resounding in the presence of a salient tension; one finally named in the final sentence – "So there's no coercion, it's totally volunta– 100 percent voluntary." This idea that prodromes are technically free to go, was repeatedly returned to throughout our interview and the SIPS training – "they're not consented to a study unless they choose to, okay?" (Interview), it depends on what "might be a choice for somebody, okay?" (Interview), participation is "always voluntary, you can withdraw at any time" (Interview), while "the 'risk assessment is free for everyone', participation 'in the clinic is not mandatory'" (Training fieldnotes), they "don't 'force' any treatment or therapy but 'offer' it" (Training fieldnotes).

Described in our interview as being presented with a "menu of options," prodromes' involvement in studies is depicted, pressed as a relatively benign process of offers and decisions. At the same time, the consistent pushing of this point as well as moving "consent" from a noun to a verb (as happened above) implied it likely that people *will* be recruited into a study. Once diagnosed prodromal, RCC explained that she will ask people, "Tell us what you want, what are you interested in, how do you want to approach your illness?" While said to illustrate that people's participation depends on what *they* want, RCC's questions also suggest that people are immediately spoken to in terms of being sick. Similarly, her description above once again suggests not only an expectation that people will be deemed prodromal but that they are called "patients." Indeed, the benevolence of the clinic is about ultimately doing what one "needs to do to treat them" – treatment is the explicit, unquestioned priority. However, this is after recognizing that the prodromal movement is technically a program of research. RCC's seamless shifting to talk of treatment illustrates a slippage in this movement between these two practices.

Yet emphasizing to people that their participation in a "study" is voluntary has a very different weight to it than emphasizing to them that their participation in "treatment" is voluntary. And being referred to as a research "participant" has a very different weight to it than being referred to as a clinical "patient." For looming over the shoulder of the treatment and patient distinctions is one's potential psychosis. When asked by one of the other trainees in the SIPS training about the "stigma" of being diagnosed prodromal, RCC replied with the following:

> The emphasis is put on "the risk" – that "we don't want to see people become worse" so will "help them to manage symptoms" so they "won't develop the illness" – "I don't have to convince you that you're at risk, I just have to convince you that you have some symptoms that need treatment – it doesn't matter how small it is" – "I never use the word 'psychosis.'"
>
> *(Training fieldnotes)*

Here RCC neutralizes concerns about diagnoses by summoning an illness from the future. Big enough to outweigh even the smallest of "symptoms," this potential threat is able to persuade people that they need treatment. And (as she described elsewhere in the SIPS training) "scary" and "stigmatized" enough to not be named; never saying "psychosis" was another recurring gesture put forth by RCC. In both the school presentation and the SIPS training she announced with some concern that the 'P' in 'SIPS' has recently been changed from 'prodromal' to 'psychosis risk' – "'I personally think that psychosis risk sounds more scary than prodrome, but I lost!'" Instead, she recommended that we describe the SIPS as "a 'risk assessment to see if people are developing a more serious mental illness' – 'If they meet the criteria, then use the word 'psychosis.'"

Thus, while initially silenced because of concerns that it may stop people from agreeing to an assessment, "psychosis" is summoned once they have been – its associated terror shifts from being harmful to helpful. When asked about the main messages that their clinic is trying to get across, RCC responded with the following:

> "There's hope for recovery," "There's treatment available," "You're not alone." You know, "If you're having these experiences just call," "Help is available." You know because I think of the stigma that's attached– I mean when you say the word "schizophrenia" to people they think horrible– [. . . . .] There's so many myths out there and misinformation and that word just scares people to death you know. [. . . . .] You know there are many people who get back a quality of life and go on to you know be in relationships and live lives, and so I think the focus– what people think of when they hear that word is the worst case scenario instead of the whole spectrum of the illness. You know and I think anything that we can do to help people recognize that is gonna be huge. You know.
>
> *(Interview)*

> Again I think for the young people– now not for the parents, but for the young people when they hear that there's so many kids that have these experiences and it doesn't mean that they're gonna develop a mental illness it just means they have to be more cautious about it, I think that's a huge relief to them. Because they know something's wrong with it, they want someone to put a name on it. "Help me with this. I know this is isn't the me I used to be. I know this is different." And people are afraid to talk to them about it. It doesn't change what they feel. They know they're different, they know something weird is going on. "So talk to me about it." You know, "Help me get over this." You know. Avoiding it doesn't make it better. Never.
>
> *(Interview)*

This extract sheds light on the "relief" that RCC consistently referred to in the trainings and our interview. That is, that the overriding response of people to the prodromal diagnosis is a sort of liberation from a hopeless sense that they were otherwise "the only ones." However, as seen above, the solution to this "stigma" is treatment – people are made to feel better about their potential illness because it is treatable. Paradoxically, it's only okay to have it because they no longer have to.

Further, people's willingness to undergo treatment is taken as a measure of their rationality – "If Dr K. wants to give me medicine and I'm paranoid I'm gonna be like, 'No way buddy. I'm not putting that in me' – everyone laughed" (Training fieldnotes), "Prodromes are far more willing to be active participants" (Training fieldnotes), "They know things are not normal. They want treatment" (Training fieldnotes), "the biggest difference between 'prodromes and schizophrenics' is that prodromes approach 'medication like a lifeline'" (Training fieldnotes), "usually psychotic people are paranoid and suspicious with regard to treatment" (School fieldnotes). Paradoxically, not wanting treatment is a sign that people *really* need it.

While above RCC neutralizes the potential stigma of being deemed prodromal with reference to people being *risky*, throughout the school presentation, the SIPS training, and our interview this neutralizing was typically done with reference to their *at-risk* status. Both relying on a looming psychosis, the former makes people dangerous whereas the latter makes them vulnerable, worthy of help:

> I think what confuses people is they think it's a diagnosis and it isn't a diagnosis it's a risk assessment. It's prevention. It's just like, you know, your risk factors for breast cancer – if your mother or your sister had breast cancer you know you're at higher risk. That's all this is about. It's about prevention. We have to assess our risk and then we have to manage it. It's not about labeling somebody, or you know taking away their hope for their future. It's giving them hope. You have these risk factors now let's look at them, lets deal with them, let's move on you know. And so I'm always surprised when people in the field have such a negative reaction to early intervention work. I'm like, "If you had a child and you knew you could probably help them mitigate at the least but maybe even prevent an illness from developing, why wouldn't you do that?"
>
> *(Interview)*

Depicting critics as confused, the diagnosis is described as risk assessment is described as prevention. RCC neutralizes concerns about the negative effects of being deemed prodromal by wrapping it in compassion and benevolence. As she said elsewhere, "I struggle with people in the field who are opposed to early work. Because it's like, 'No this isn't about stigmatizing somebody or traumatizing them.' It's about, 'Okay you're at higher risk, what can we do to minimize that?'" (Interview).

Saying this approach is "just like" the one taken with breast cancer further establishes it as logical vis-à-vis the authority of 'hard' Science – engaging as it does with a (supposedly) indisputable flesh. Similarly, RCC started both the school presentation and the SIPS training with a wry reference to her title slide – "A Revolutionary Approach to Treating Psychosis: Identifying Young People Early" – that the movement is not actually *that* revolutionary:

> RCC continued that while this may be a "revolutionary approach" in mental health, the notion of "an at-risk phase" has been around with regard to physical health "for a long time." She drew on the diabetes example, talking though the different stages of identification and intervention that people experience before they are given insulin. In a similar way, if a young person is diagnosed prodromal it "of course" does not mean that they will be given anti-psychotics. They will at first try a range of therapies, like family and cognitive, and then try herbal medicines like glycerin and amino acids.
>
> *(School fieldnotes)*

Thus, contrary to accusations, a risk assessment gives people hope for their future by allowing them to have some control over their pending illness – aka treatment. Drawing it on the whiteboard for me before everyone else arrived at the SIPS training, and citing it later that day as the second "most important thing" in RCC's practice (the first being psychoeducation), RCC is referring here to their "3-stage line of intervention." The "early prodrome" is given "softer" interventions (such as supportive, cognitive behavioral or family therapy); the "mid-prodrome" is given more "naturalistic" interventions (such as herbal medicines); and the "late prodrome" is given "low-dose antipsychotics." Now neutralizing critiques that the movement may be recklessly prescribing anti-psychotics, the incremental structure of this model renders the prevention approach even more trustworthy.

During our interview, RCC went into more detail about their use of antipsychotics, emphasizing that while "a lot of people in the field have very strong feelings about– against using antipsychotic medications you know," "you don't start there" – "if you can hold it or have it at bay with something else of course you would do that. But if it keeps progressing and getting worse and worse at some point you do have to consider medication treatment":

> You always wanna start with the least invasive thing. And you know– But that doesn't always work and you need to have this whole arsenal.

> You know my analogy is– Nobody wants to fight a war, but when you're fighting a mental health war, you're not just gonna fight it with a hand gun. You're gonna use every weapon in your arsenal available. So you start with the least invasive tools and you work your way up. But you need to know what's available. You know you need to know what are best practices, you need to know what are evidence-based treatments so that you can help you know people.
>
> *(Interview)*

Described as on the frontlines of a "mental health war," the prevention approach shifts from helping an individual to carrying out a civil duty. "It" – psychosis – is an increasingly aggressive force that "of course" warrants increasingly aggressive intervention if it can't otherwise be held "at bay." Once again building an intensity through repetition ("You need to know . . ."), the prodrome is depicted as having an enemy within; one so devious and dangerous that it requires "every weapon in your arsenal." Made in the shadow of a future attack on self or others, one's 'choice' to engage in treatment is effectively mandated – detained by the threat of future psychosis, available to be searched for evidence of a pending pathology, for data.

Search

> So my bottom line is always: Are we getting the help to the people who need it? You know and our clinic is free, so the fact that there's not a DSM-5 code doesn't impact us cos we're not billing. But a mental health clinic – without having a code for billing, how are they gonna give this person good treatment, you know what I mean? They're gonna have to give them treatment under– some other treatment that wouldn't be the specialized treatment that we know would help them for this. So I feel sad about that because I think it denies people the best care you know. And that doesn't please me. But again it's not because I want them to have a name or a label, it's because I want them to get the treatment that we know is evidence-based.
>
> *(Interview)*

> You know right now what drug company's gonna put a lot of money into whether or not a medication is effective with prodromes when nobody can bill for a prodrome? You know so, it's true and you know a huge issue when a prodrome gets to the state where they're really pretty severe– having severe symptoms, and it looks like antipsychotic medication is wanted. It's a huge question: How long do they need to

be on the medication? We can't do any of that you know now. We don't know. You know so we know with chronic schizophrenics they usually have to stay on medication the rest of their life. We don't know that about the prodrome. And we're never gonna get there if we can't research it. You know. So it does tie your hands. You know because when you're a treater, when you're out there in clinical practice, you want to do evidence-based practice. But somebody's got to get the evidence you know [chuckles] and it's– you know it's very difficult.

(Interview)

These extracts followed RCC's frustration in our interview that, "people doing early intervention work didn't want it in the DSM! I was like, 'Help me understand?!'" She unequivocally counters any critiques of the prodromal movement with people "getting the help they need." The "specialized treatment" offered by her clinic is filling a "sad" gap left by the lack of an official diagnosis in the context of a US health system dependent on insurance companies *and* undoing knots tied by a US research system dependent on drug companies. Ultimately concerned that people are being denied "the best care," RCC thus pushes a benevolence that orbits around "evidence-based treatment."

And yet, at the same time, this evidence base is undermined by this very same benevolence. During the SIPS training RCC spoke of how "the conversion rate has now dropped to 30 percent 'because of course it's not ethical to not treat.'" In conveying this supposed common sense, she also highlights a complexity in the prodromal movement; recalling that this treatment is preventative, that it is intervening on a future threat. If people are treated then this threat can never be falsified, we do not know if the prodromal diagnosis was actually a false positive, one's potential psychosis is eternal. Paradoxically, the treatment that drives this scientific program of research simultaneously interferes with its scientific logic.

Similarly, during both the SIPS training and the school presentation RCC described how the "lot of luck" that their clinic had with an anti-psychotic meant that they were *not* able to collect the evidence that they need:

> Further data is needed regarding the efficacy of medication, "unfortunately our clinic is part of the reason for that" – they undertook a 2-year study titrating patients onto an anti-psychotic – starting them at 5mg and increasing by 5mg/week – found that 15mg was the "magic bullet" that "eliminated symptoms" in the prodrome – "patients did fabulously" – at one year they were supposed to titrate them off to see "how long the benefit might last for when given medication prophylactically" – "guess what happened? None of our

patients would go off it. They said, "I'm sorry but I'm not going to risk going off medication."

(Training fieldnotes)

They have not yet issued medication guidelines because they do not have the evidence about how long the prodrome should be on medication for, versus "chronic schizophrenics who have to take medication for the rest of their lives." "Unfortunately, our clinic is one of the reasons": they were given the task to figure out "how long is long enough" and undertook a study that involved titrating the prodrome onto and then off a drug. In doing so they found the "magic bullet" that held the prodrome for a year," but then when they went to titrate people off it they refused to go off saying "I don't want to be sick again" and that even if their clinic just went ahead and stopped them taking the drugs they would just go to their doctor and get a prescription themselves.

(School fieldnotes)

Said with a tongue-in-cheek tone, this reason for their clinic "unfortunately" contributing to the lack of data and guidelines on prodromal drug treatment was recounted by RCC with pride. Revealing and outdoing the limitations of clinical trial requirements, the movement was once more placed on the side of 'the people.' Moreover, their 'unsuccessful' study proved exactly what the clinic believes in and pushes for – that the "patients did fabulously." During the SIPS training we were told that anti-psychotics are "'amazing'" – "'after 8 weeks they are better,'" symptoms "'go like that,'" people "'won't stop taking them'." Moreover, while a recurring trope in psychopharmacology, by describing one drug as "the magic bullet" RCC once more positions psychosis as an aggressive, prowling illness to be impeded, if not shot, by antipsychotics.

Thus prodromal research is – as RCC put it in the previous section – a "tricky field." Unable to "bring them all to my consciousness" earlier in our interview, here RCC has found the list of ten studies that her clinic was conducting:

We have the NAPLS-3 obviously. We have the double-blind placebo-controlled over-the-counter drug study. We have specialized treatment for the prodrome, so our clinic treatment versus usual care, so what somebody might get if they went to a community psychiatrist as opposed to somebody who specializes in early intervention. There are some– we're floating some screeners, questionnaires that people feel might be helpful in identifying people who are at risk and comparing

> how they score on the questionnaire with how they score on the SIPS and is it really valid. So we have two of those [. . . . .] So you know we have various studies. Right now we do not have a medication trial. Sometimes we do. We just finished up a double-blind placebo-controlled trial with an antipsychotic, but right now we're not offering a medication study.
>
> (Interview)

As mentioned in the previous section, this list is typically described as a "menu of options" for prodromes to choose from. However, elsewhere in our interview RCC also spoke of how it brings the "complicated" demand of "dividing up the people who are prodromal into the different studies" – shifting the locus of decision-making from the young person to the researcher. As she explains:

> Through the process of the SIPS you know you learn about the person, so you know they're pro-meds, they're anti-meds, they're this, they're that. So then at the end when I'm reporting back to them on my findings with the SIPS I'll bring up the studies that I think they would most respond to, with the caveat these aren't the only studies.
>
> (Interview)

Openly tailoring the "options" that she presents to people as per those that they will "most respond to," RCC is implying positively that they individualize people's treatment plans. And yet there is also no suggestion that people will not be involved in any of these studies.

Indeed, even when people are technically *not* enrolled in a treatment study, RCC always makes sure they have some kind of intervention. During the SIPS training she described how, as opposed to when she first joined the movement and they "didn't do anything, just watched and listened," now "'no one will walk out of here without at least psychoeducation.'" A similar commitment was announced with pride during the school presentation as RCC told us that after a few years of doing this work "'it no longer felt ethical to just watch and follow along. We now feel we have to help them to have a shot at getting better' – so they increased their clinical treatment component of the project." Met with what I noted as "noises of approval," this promise to educate/treat was received as a progress that trumps Science with compassion, that puts young people's 'needs' first.

In the following extracts from our interview, RCC goes into more detail about what this progress looks like in practice:

The early warning signs and the things that you can do to you know reduce it– to reduce your stress and manage your stress and keep yourself healthy. You know when we go through the things with people and, you know especially adolescents, "How much water do you drink a day?" [Said slowly, with a 'detective' tone, laughing] You know they're horrible! You know they just don't drink water at all. And we encourage them, you know, just start with one extra glass a day and see if that makes a difference. And they all come back and go, "I'm not as tired, I'm not as lethargic, I can think clearer." They don't realize that they're just on that edge of dehydration and it really impacts their functioning. You know, getting good sleep you know, they just– all of these things contribute to them having better physical health and mental health. So each little tool that you give them really helps them to improve you know. And, of course, I mean you know there has to be psychoeducation about substance abuse because so many of the young people self-medicate you know. And they think temporarily in the moment it helps them feel better and it's really hard to make them understand that ultimately they're doing themselves a disservice because ultimately it makes it worse, not better, you know. And when I talk with young people I'm very honest about it – "Look you got a raw deal, there's no doubt about it. Eight of your friends can smoke pot and be fine. Unfortunately, because of your genetic make-up, you can't. And you just have to accept that you know? It's like a diabetic can't eat sugar. You know it's like, is it fair? No of course not but it's a fact and you have to face it."

(Interview)

RCC: So there are assessments that we do. And then the other part would be their therapy – whether they were doing individual therapy or family focused therapy or whatever. So then it would be that piece of that.

Me: Right. So people would always have both, always have the therapy component?

RCC: Well we encourage them. We can't force them but we certainly encourage them to have some type of supported therapy. And even with the patients who refuse supportive therapy, we do the assessments in a [pause] supportive therapy way. So even though we're doing an assessment if we know they haven't signed on for treatment we'll do psychoeducation in that, and we'll do some therapy. You know, "Oh so how did you deal with that when it happened? How'd that work for you? Oh it didn't work, so well what do you think you could different?" You know? So even though it's supposed to be an assessment if we know they haven't signed on for therapy we will incorporate that piece of psychoeducation and therapy.

(Interview)

Directly following a claim that, "If we can catch them sooner then their quality of life is so altered you know. It really is," in the former extract RCC is effectively explaining how psychoeducation detains the prodrome. Combining Science, compassion, and a 'straight-up' kind of approach, these "little tools" are carried by a truthiness and a trustworthiness that gives them an authority. Harmless, everyday, and common sense, they are difficult to refuse. Yet, taken in a context of trying to convince someone that they are at-risk for a serious mental illness, that they may develop psychosis if they don't do something about it, they are a lot stickier than they seem. Routinely surveilled by others and and/or themselves, the abnormality and threat of people's psyches is salient. Spun into a prodrome, their potential psychosis is never far away, waiting.

Regular, intensive interactions also occur through the actual study protocols. In our interview, RCC explained how being enrolled in a treatment study means coming to the clinic anything between once a week and once a month, while being enrolled in a naturalistic study is slightly less – the NAPLS-3 protocol described in the second extract below, for example, will mean coming in once every two months:

RCC: Yup so if they're in a treatment study they would come in and obviously the first thing we're gonna check on is are they having any side effects, you know, we wanna make sure that the treatment we're giving them, if it's a medication or supplement, is not having any negative impact on them.

Me: And that's about sitting down and chatting with them about how it's going?

RCC: And taking blood and you know doing side effect assessment scales, things like that. Then we'll also monitor the progression and the symptoms because that's very important, we need to know 'Is the intervention working?' you know. So we have to monitor– so we do the SOPS[7]– repeated and you know check on that. Other scales, Calgary Depression Scale,[8] you know. In NAPLS we did stressful life events because we know stress has such an impact on the illness, so we'd monitor what their stress levels were like. Depression scales, anxiety scales. So we really do the total clinical picture okay, and monitor how that's doing.

(Interview)

RCC: Looking at the assessment list that we have to do it's gonna be– those visits are gonna be well over an hour. They will be you know absolutely over an hour because the saliva testing is over a two-hour period.
Me: What is the saliva testing for?
RCC: Cortisol – that hormone that we talked about?
Me: The stress one?
RCC: Yeah so, they spit in a test tube. Not much, like this much [indicates a few millimeters with fingers] and– at baseline when they first come in. Then we work on the assessments and then at the one-hour point they do it again. We keep doing assessments and then at the two-hour point they do it again. And so we measure their cortisol levels. And you know there's some prep work that has to be done for that, there's some dietary restrictions – they have to avoid caffeine, nicotine, and dairy.

(Interview)

Here, RCC describes what happens during visits for a treatment and naturalistic study, respectively. As well as the abovementioned dietary restrictions required the night before these assessments, people are also encouraged to "refrain as much as you can" from using "substances"/"abusing drugs" for the entire time that they are enrolled in a study. Not to mention that, if they are considered 'mid' or 'late' prodrome, they will also be asked to ingest a psychoactive substance every day.

Once inside, RCC went on to say that each visit can take up to two and a half hours of psychometric scales, taking blood, saliva sampling, and – as described elsewhere in our interview – neurocognitive testing and brain scans. Searched for telltale flesh by a desire to extract one's "individual risk," and thus to calculate it:

It takes all of the risk factors and your individual ranking. So, "You have first degree relatives, so you get this okay. You scored this on the SOPS, you get this okay. You were physically abused as a child so you have a history of trauma, okay." Now mine, "I don't have a first degree relative, I get nothing in that area. But I have this score on the SOPS. And I don't have any trauma, so I get nothing there." So it's not looking at the general population's risk it's looking at your individual risk and how each of those factors weighs in – your biochemistry, your cortisol levels, your brain– your grey matter. You know everything is taken into consideration and, "Now I can tell you your individual risk." That's gonna be phenomenal when this comes to fruition.

(Interview)

In the "hard" absence of "that definitive blood test that we can give that says 'You're gonn– You're psychotic,'" the prodromal movement is turning to "identifying all the biomarkers that alert us to something going on you know" (Interview) – the tiniest of signs with which a trained eye or latest technology can detect future psychosis. In our interview, as well as in the school presentation, and the SIPS training, RCC excitedly described their ostensibly futuristic risk calculator that, as mentioned in Chapter 2, has since been released. Drawing on the algorithms produced through the NAPLS-2 data, the 'Individualized Risk Calculator' estimates the likelihood that a young person diagnosed as prodromal will become psychotic within two years with an accuracy said to be comparable to those used for cardiovascular disease and cancer[9].

Fuel

After being captured and interrogated by *nets* and *borderguards*, prodromes are held in prodromal *custody* through the threat of psychosis and *searched* by studies for those parts of their experiences, lives, or flesh that point toward this imminent illness. Operating within the fertile US landscape of insurance and research industries, these four cogs produce a coordinated set of little pieces that can be distributed across North America and put back together as algorithms to predict psychosis, exemplifying the workings of a control society. Oscillating between quotas and calculators, they allow the movement to feed itself with its own risk factors, to produce its own fuel for data production.

Thus, this prodromal movement works as a prodrome machine, making the fuel to make the data to make the fuel to make the data to. . . Relentlessly spinning, its cogs not only overcome that principle obstacle to making a powerful worldwide movement: sample size. As scientific operations they also defend the movement against that infernal alternative that threatens it: that people's experiences are Normal. As perhaps epitomized by RCC's repeated stating of "you know" in her interview, this machine is lubricated with a common sense that is made from urgency, trust, and compassion. To suggest that people's experiences are Normal is to cause another Sandy Hook, to deny that Science knows best, to be complicit in stigma, to take away hope, to ignore what people want, to deny people's expertise, to be irrational, to not be on the side of 'the people,' to not recognize the benefits of treatment, to be unethical. In short, it is non-sense. This non-sense allows the infernal alternative to mobilize the movement at increasing speeds, loudly whirring, unable to hear cries that something else is possible. In this way a wall is built around the prodrome. Blocking critique and demarcating a territory for prodrome production, this wall generates increasing evidence that people's experiences are *not* Normal – protecting the movement, protecting America.

Notes

1 I use 'Normal' as shorthand for non-pathological as it evokes the status quo and as such comes thick with politics, power, and a tendency to morph across different contexts, making it a particularly threatening infernal alternative.
2 The following four sections draw upon fieldnotes and materials that I gathered during a one-hour Community Presentation (henceforth, 'school presentation') on the prodrome at a middle school and a one-day Rater Training on the Structured Interview of Psychosis-Risk Syndromes (SIPS) at a prodromal clinic (henceforth, 'SIPS training') – both of which were held in December 2014. I was invited to both events by the facilitator, whom I had emailed about my research into the prodromal movement, stating that this had in part derived from a broader interest on the intersections of psychiatry and security. Both of these events were affiliated with the same prodromal clinic and facilitated by the same person – a Research Clinical Coordinator (henceforth, RCC) – whom I also had a 1:1 90-minute semi-structured interview with on the morning following the SIPS training. Thus, this chapter also draws on the transcript from this interview. During the school presentation and the SIPS training I introduced myself to other participants as a PhD candidate from the City University of New York who was doing an ethnography of the prodromal movement, and sat at the front to the right hand side of the projection, taking notes by hand that tried to capture as many direct quotes as possible. The interview was audio-recorded and I also took notes by hand. Immediately after all three of these events I typed up my notes, integrating them with their affiliated materials/audio-recording, removing or replacing identifying detail, fleshing them out with as much sensory information that I could recall, and adding any nascent analytic insights. Alongside mapping the mechanics of the movement, I focused on what was happening *in between* – what moments felt like, what was made by claims' adjacency, my own and others' embodied responses, what 'else' was evoked, things that seemed to come 'out of nowhere' thus alluding to the presence of other arguments or audiences, unexpected collisions of affect, things that seemed contradictory or oddly recurring. The theoretical lens through which I viewed and arranged the data was informed by not only my engagement with critical race and critical security studies, but my concurrent involvement in activism against the New York Police Department for the racism of their 'stop and frisk' practices (see Liebert, 2017b). For all quotes and extracts I have changed identifying information and removed stutters and 'um's. While I typically only cite one extract in order to make my argument, it is important to note that the content across the school presentation, SIPS training, and RCC interview was highly repetitive, even verbatim – strongly implying that I was encountering a script. This felt particularly significant given that, as said to me by an assistant director of another prodrome clinic during a phone conversation, the role of RCC's clinic has made the worldwide prodromal movement "an American thing." Indeed, I was told by RCC during one of our breaks in the SIPS training that she was increasingly being asked to do trainings outside of the US. Thus, the words that follow not only circulate through RCC's clinic, but the US and beyond.
3 Yet, evoking a familiar pattern, RCC's use of "mis-diagnosis" may also be misleading: the rise in evidence that antidepressants can cause suicidality came with increased claims that these drugs exacerbated an underlying depression (Liebert & Gavey, 2009), and the rise in evidence that antidepressants can cause mania came with increased claims that these drugs exacerbated an underlying bipolar disorder (Liebert, 2013b).

4 'Disease-mongering' describes the tactics used by drug companies to create markets for their products, including direct to consumer advertising, 'education' campaigns, and 'consultations' with diagnostic professionals (Moynihan & Cassels, 2005).
5 In the SIPS, the five 'positive symptoms' of psychosis are referred to as 'P1' through 'P5' – 'Unusual thought content/Delusional ideas', 'Suspiciousness/Persecutory ideas', 'Grandiose ideas', 'Perceptual abnormalities/Hallucinations', and 'Disorganised communication' respectively. These are rated between zero and six, with 0 meaning the symptom is 'absent', 1 'questionably present', 2 'mild', 3 'moderate', 4 'moderately severe', 5 'severe but not psychotic', and 6 'severe and psychotic'.
6 Institutional Review Board, which determines the ethicality of research.
7 'Scale of Prodromal Symptoms', which has been incorporated into the SIPS.
8 Also known as the CDSS, or 'Calgary Depression Scale for Schizophrenia.'
9 See Tyrone Cannon and colleagues (2016).

DRAWING 3. "Seeping." Black ink on cochineal print, el Jardín Etnobotánico de Oaxaca. Rachel Jane Liebert, 2016.

PLATE 1. "Craigslist's Missed Connections," *Missed Connections*, New York City, United States, 2015. Screenshot by Rachel Jane Liebert.

PLATE 2. "I have never doubted that my dreams are the products of my own mind (false)," *Missed Connections*, New York City, United States, 2015. Photo by Holli McEntegart.

PLATE 3. "Good luck charms don't work (false)," *Missed Connections*, New York City, United States, 2015. Photo by Holli McEntegart.

PLATE 4. "The hand motions that strangers make seem to influence me at times (true)," *Missed Connections*, New York City, United States, 2015. Photo by Holli McEntegart.

PLATE 5. "I have noticed sounds on my records that are not there at other times (true)," *Missed Connections*, Tamaki Makaurau Auckland, Aotearoa New Zealand, 2015. Photo by Olivia Holmes.

PLATE 6. "The hand motions that strangers make seem to influence me at times (true)," *Missed Connections,* Tamaki Makaurau Auckland, Aotearoa New Zealand, 2015. Photo by Olivia Holmes.

PLATE 7. "I have had the momentary feeling that someone's place has been taken by a look-a-like (true)," *Missed Connections*, Tamaki Makaurau Auckland, Aotearoa New Zealand, 2015. Photo by Olivia Holmes.

PLATE 8. "It is not possible to harm others merely by thinking bad thoughts about them (false)," *Missed Connections*, Tamaki Makaurau Auckland, Aotearoa New Zealand, 2015. Photo by Olivia Holmes.

4
COILS

In the previous chapter I described the cogs of a machine that, making fuel for continued data production, works to protect both the prodromal movement and 'America.' These discursive and non-discursive mechanisms suggest the workings of what Gilles Deleuze and Felix Guattari (1987) call a 'molar assemblage' – an extensive multiplicity of heterogeneous elements organized into a hierarchical system with a center of significance and subjectification: the Prodrome. The first two cogs, *nets* and *borderguards*, mark a boundary around the prodrome, enclosing a field of interiority that is fixed and stabilized through the second two cogs, *custody* and *search*. This prodromal territory is characterized by a rigid segmentation whereby young people's experiences, lives, and flesh are divided into predetermined parts and organized as prodromal. This machine thus mimics the dominant image of 'progress' within a neocolonial security state; one that Isabelle Stengers (2012) describes as "a hierarchical figure of a tree, with Science as its trunk" (p. 2). Such 'Science' – in the singular and with a big 'S' – emerged during colonization as, "a general conquest bent on translating everything that exists into objective, rational knowledge" (p. 2). 'Bent on' because this conquest – operating through an assemblage – is animated by desire. Drawing the above cogs also outlines the affective flows circulating in and through the prodrome machine. In this chapter I map these coils, the contours of the serpent characterizing a control society. To do so, I first consider their Scientific legacy.

Legacy

Desire to Know

Coloniality is dependent on a hierarchy of Knowing, Knowers, Knowledge. As documented by Trinh Minh-ha (1989), Gayatri Spivak (1988), Linda Tuhiwai Smith (1999), among many others, those who colonized established themselves as those who had access to the Truth and the colonized as, quite simply, those who did not. Fooled by their 'savage' beliefs, they needed guidance-*cum*-violence – even, or perhaps especially, if they did not 'know' this themselves. For Sylvia Wynter (2003) this relation of power is based on an "ethnoclass (i.e., Western bourgeois) conception of the human, Man" (p. 260); one that bought the world of modernity into existence from the fifteenth century onwards, is now at the center of this world, and demands the subordination of the "empirical human world" (p. 262) – those peoples whose gender, sexuality, nation, ethnicity, race, class, and/or disability exist to the side of Man.

This shift from human to Man began when Western intellectuals began what Wynter calls the *de-supernaturalizing* of modes of being the former. Prior to this collision, societies explicitly mapped ideas about being human onto ideas about the cosmos, experiencing them as a supernatural, extrahuman 'objective set of facts' that gave rise to, demanded a particular social order. These worlds-*cum*-directives – what Wynter calls 'adaptive truth-fors' – were thus both absolute and particular. In contrast, the West's intellectuals mapped the idea of order onto 'natural laws' – freeing the 'objective set of facts' into something 'out there,' repressing any recognition of social reality being locally, collectively produced. Now seen in universal terms, the world as an entirety became Knowable. Bringing with it a "drive to final mastery" that fortified the expansionist exploration and attempted colonization of the globe (Sandoval, 2000). To Know was and is to capture, own, control – whether ideas, plants, peoples, or lands.

Wynter (2003) describes how this de-supernaturalization led to the description of two kinds of human-as-Man. First, the human of the evangelizing mission of the Church, or 'Man1,' a Christian subject who dominated from the Renaissance to the eighteenth century; second, the human of the imperializing mission of the state, or 'Man2,' a political subject who accompanied the ensuing territorial expansion and conquest. This move from Man1 to Man2 marked a shift of the idea of order away from spiritual toward rational im/perfection. As Wynter summarizes, "if God made everything for mankind then he would have had to make it according to rational, non-arbitrary rules that could be knowable by the beings that He made it for" (p. 278). Going from supernatural to natural causation, emancipating Man as one who can Know, thus prepared the ground for Science. This new mode of Knowing required the making, disregarding, and exterminating of a physical referent for its irrational or sub-rational other – whether the 'witches' of Europe (Federici, 2014) or the 'barbarians' of the New World (Kelley, 2000). Such making, disregarding, and exterminating was facilitated in particular by 'social' Science (Tuhiwai Smith, 1999), thrusting 'objects' of inquiry into categories, and spinning them into a hierarchy; a 'thingification' that not only involved a destruction of the intellectual and cultural contributions of the colonized (Césaire, 1955) but the vitality of, and our solidarity with, the cosmos and flesh (Federici, 2014). In turn, being "enslaved to one's passions," to irrationality, was to become a signifier of threat – whether seen as incivility or illness (Wynter, 2003). The colonial emergence of Man and Science thus also provided the conditions of possibility for modern-day conceptions of madness.

Ignorance

Come the mid-twentieth century and decolonial movements were powerfully contesting the circulation of this Western rationality, understanding and revealing it as an 'ethnophilosophy' (Sandoval, 2000) – indeed its own adaptive truth-for. Nonetheless, to date Science has by and large not attended to the peculiarity and coloniality of its worldview – Psychology included (Adams, Dobles, Gomez, Kurtis & Molin, 2015). This repression, according to Wynter (2003), is necessary for the maintenance of Man and his world – we must, "make opaque to themselves/ourselves . . . the empirical fact of our ongoing production and reproduction of our order, of its genre of being human" (p. 307). It follows that Western intellectuals continue to be the agents of the de-supernaturalization that created us. Stengers (2012) describes this history as an "anonymity that inhabits us and constitutes us, still and again, as 'the thinking head of humanity'" (p. 15). An "anonymity" because to believe this betrays an inability to see the role that "we" play in knowing and thus that all ideas are partial and local, that there is "non-knowing at the heart of all knowledge" (p. 3). As Trinh (1989) writes, "The civilized man has become a problem to the civilized man, and he who shows himself naked with his speech or says out loud that the emperor has no clothes should expect his peers to call him an exhibitionist" (p. 60).

To show oneself naked is to reveal that one's knowledge is bounded by their flesh; a flashing that feels particularly vulnerable given that it not only threatens (one's place atop) a hierarchy of Knowing, Knowers, Knowledge but exposes the violence on which this hierarchy depended and depends. As Aimé Césaire (1955) argues, colonization itself ironically works, "to *decivilize* the colonizer, to *brutalize* him in the true sense of the world, to degrade him, to awaken him to buried instincts, to covetousness, violence, race hatred, and moral relativism" (p. 35, his emphasis). This "regression" infects colonizers and spreads outwards until "a poison has been distilled into the veins of Europe and, slowly but surely, the continent proceeds toward *savagery*" (p. 36, his emphasis). And, at the same time, ". . . his brain functions after the fashion of certain elementary types of digestive systems, it filters. And the filter lets through only what can nourish the thick skin of the bourgeois' clear conscience" (p. 52). Unable to justify itself with reason or conscience, this "forgetting machine" thus enables the West to "take refuge in a hypocrisy" (p. 31). That is, the idea that colonization was civilization, both driving and proving an inherent superiority.

Wynter's opacity, Stengers' anonymity, Trinh's clothes, Césaire's filter, then, point to an ignorance that capacitates present-day white supremacy. One that takes the standpoint of the propertied white male as given (Mills, 2007); this "epistemological crisis" was and is nourished within capitalism (Mignolo, 2012), which depends on a hierarchical relation between a subject and its property, necessitating an ignorance of the latter's vitality, whether peoples or lands. By looking through ignorance without seeing it, white supremacy "insulates itself against refutation" (Mills, 2007, p. 19), justifying a racist status quo, spiraling into deeper and deeper ignorance. From this perspective, whiteness is characterized by an alienation that is both "duping and duped" (Fanon, 1952, p. 17), making white people that are "at once the perpetrator and the victim of a delusion" (p. 175). Meanwhile – as Gloria Anzaldúa (1987) describes the effects of this "whitewashing" on people of color – the "dominant white culture is killing us slowly with its ignorance" (p. 108).

Fear of 'regressing'

Thus it became "*unthinkable* to accept the idea that a knowing subject was possible beyond the subject of knowledge postulated by the very concept of rationality put in place by modern epistemology" (Mignolo, 2012, p. 442, my emphasis). European thinkers have become locked into their worldview, trapped in a colonial episteme (Dabashi, 2015). And yet haunted. Decolonial scholars have long documented how a lingering sense of the violence and limits of this episteme also drives the continued policing of borders between the colonized and the colonizers (e.g., Memmi, 1957, 1991). This residue manifests in intangible, unspeakable, unreasonable ways. It is felt. A ghostly 'absence' that rises up to protect ignorance, and thus whiteness, when it is threatened by knowledge. As Nelson Maldonado-Torres (2016) writes,

...true anxiety over death emerges for the normative subjects of the zone of being human (e.g., the white) when they consider, not their individual death, but the complete de-legitimation and the end of their world.

(p. 14)

In contemporary anti-racist activism this phenomenon is known as 'white fragility.' Raising de/colonization solicits, "indifference, obfuscation, constant evasion and aggression" – whether in "the guise of neutral and rational assessments, post-racialism, and well-intentioned liberal values" (Maldonado-Torres, 2016, p. 8) or "psychic wounds" that work to mask privilege and history, normalize violence, defend the status quo, and anesthetize individuals from painful knowledge (Watkins & Shulman, 2008). When white supremacy shakes, white people shake.

Frantz Fanon (1952) depicts this fragility in his description of the white man's "affective ankylosis," a "total inability to liquidate the past once and for all" as there is a "white world" in the way (p. 92). This white world is white ignorance, buttressed by a fearful sense that constricts a capacity to feel, our poisoned blood vessels, as to do so will reveal the hypocrisy – the violence, the torture, the genocide – that feeds white lives. For if we felt, we would witness our own regression: "Uprooted, pursued, baffled, doomed to watch the dissolution of the truths that he has worked out for himself one after another, he has to give up projecting onto the world an antinomy that co-exists with him" (p. 2). That is, that perhaps we do not Know so much after all.

Indeed, for Stengers (2012), fears that one might – and thus moral imperatives that one shall not – regress to soft Illusory 'beliefs' lying far from the hard Truth of 'progress' torment the abovementioned Science, "bent on translating everything that exists into objective, rational knowledge" (p. 2). Fanon (1952) articulates a similar dynamic:

> I embrace the world! I am the world! The white man has never understood this magic substitution. The white man wants the world; he wants it for himself alone. He finds himself predestined master of this world. He enslaves it. An acquisitive relation is established between the world and him. But there exist other values that fit only my forms. Like a magician, I robbed the white man of "a certain world," forever after lost to him and his. When that happened the white man must have been rocked backward by a force that he could not identify, so little used as he is to such reactions. Somewhere beyond the object world of farms and banana trees and rubber trees, I had subtly bought

the real world into being. The essence of the world was my fortune. Between the world and me a relation of coexistence was established. I had discovered the primeval One. My "speaking hands" tore at the hysterical throat of the world. The white man had the anguished feeling that I was escaping from him and that I was taking something with me. He went through my pockets. He thrust probes into the least circumvolution of my brain. Everywhere he found only the obvious. So it was obvious I had a secret.

(p. 97)

Embracing the world, being the world, disrupts the hierarchy insisted by capitalism and colonization, creating a fear of 'regressing' that provokes a desire to Know. White ignorance is taunted by Fanon's secret, by the incapacity of Science to find anything beyond what it is looking for, what it can see. For Trinh (1989), this manifests as a "positivist yearning for transparency":

> . . . as if thinker could be conceived apart from thought and beyond it; as if science which comes about through the element of discourse could simply cross over discourse and create a world of its own without giving up the series of rational and empirical operations that make it up.
>
> *(p. 64)*

In order to continue, Science must dismiss, ignore the very operations on which it builds the world, its world. Like the emperor's clothes, like white ignorance, the Truth of these operations is in their 'transparency,' in being seen-through and unseen.

And, as the history of colonization demonstrates, this positivist yearning requires not just an ignorance but a destruction of other possible worlds. Philippe Pignarre and Isabelle Stengers (2011) propose that this is *the* mode of contemporary capitalism, which is mobilized by the production of 'infernal alternatives' – those other ways of engaging with phenomena that must be destroyed so as not to threaten the truthiness of the status quo. Like coloniality, this dynamic has poisoned us all, placing us on the defensive, not open to an otherness. Infernal alternatives thus collaborate with ignorance, as both block an acknowledgement of difference, of things being able to be another way, of the instability and thus open possibility of Truth. As experimented with in the previous chapter, it is these infernal alternatives that also mobilize Science, which establishes a set of operations that protect its Truth and thus the hierarchy of Knowing, Knowers, Knowledge on which it resides. Psychology included. For Derek Hook (2012), psy attempts to understand, make predictable and generate knowledge about "others" are "as much that of a social science as of fantasy, as much, in other words of a social scientific 'will to know' as of an affective economy of fear/desire" (p. 160). In turn, these attempts spiral into Truth, obscuring their shaky, violent assumptions.

Paranoia

Thus *desire-to-know* is entangled with *fear-of-regressing*. Yet, within conditions of coloniality, each enflames the other, given that the hierarchy of Knowing, Knowers, Knowledge depends on an ignoring of worldly vitality, Indigenous capacity, colonial violence, the primordial unknown, and white supremacy. Desire-to-know threatens this ignorance, activating a fear-of-regressing, intensifying desire-to-know . . . : a spiraling dis-ease that I read as 'paranoia.'

The circular nature of paranoia has been explicitly identified by a number of scholars (e.g., Butler, 1993; Cromby & Harper, 2012; Sedgwick, 2003). However, Dave Harper (2008) also offers an account of paranoia as an experience of "knowing too much" that can be situated within a sense of precarity – "people in powerless positions may adopt paranoid beliefs . . . because it makes sense in a world where others really do have power over you" (p. 7). While in this quote Harper is referring to people who are marginalized in terms of class or ethnicity, it also makes sense when one considers the above described ignorance and fragility of white supremacy. This dynamic appears to be circulating between the lines of Stephen Frosh (2016) who suggests we live in "a paranoid-inducing world" whereby "the frame that is meant to support us turns against us, in ways that we cannot even be sure of, so we end up mistrusting everything" (p. 14). Despite (or perhaps because of[1]) drawing on Fanon, whiteness is the unspoken norm in Frosh's analysis, whose undefined "us" and "we" implies a universality and whose description of the "visible invisibility" of surveillance ("visible at least since the Edward Snowden revelations; invisible because we simply don't know how far it all goes," p. 15) ignores the very visible policing of poor, female, trans, brown, and black communities happening within the same regime. Both of which reveal a whiteness between the lines, of the "frame that is meant to support us," of the America that one wants to be made great again.[2]

Indeed, in her reading of the Rodney King beating,[3] Judith Butler (1993) writes of how a white paranoia structures the ways in which one is able to *see* violence in the US – shifting, in this case, threat onto the figure of the black man and off police; the former seen as threatening, the latter – protecting whiteness – not. In doing so paranoia shields the "virgin sanctity" of whiteness, while lubricating a repeated and ritualistic production of blackness. Splitting intentionality away from whiteness and investing it into blackness, paranoia thus constitutes a racist imaginary that enables white people to always believe they are in danger, completing the circle[4]: a desire-to-know the 'enemy' entangles with a fear-of-regressing, a refusal to witness the violence of whiteness, making paranoia. Ghassan Hage (2003) invites coloniality into this spiraling image. He documents a paranoiac colonial sensibility in Australia that is based on a fear of losing, or never attaining, the superiority promised by whiteness; one that was sustained by immigration and enflamed by 9/11. In Australia, a settler colony, this paranoia has been a "potent political force," a "colonized political will trying to reassert its sovereignty over all or part of the territory" (p. 418); one that is animated by a fear of decolonization. As Hage writes, "the core element of Australia's colonial paranoia is a fear of loss of Europeanness or whiteness and the lifestyle and privileges that are seen to emanate directly from them" (p. 419). Hage thus argues that there is an "excessively fragile conception of the self" underpinning paranoia (p. 419), particularly for working class whites. A fragility that is amplified by a nearby knowing that colonization depended on genocide, that the natural environment is uncontrollable, and that there is 'uncivilized' otherness all around.

Similarly, although writing from England – the germ of the British empire – Sanjay Sharma and Ashwani Sharma (2003) and Ashwani Sharma (2009) document how, in the wake of a century of increasing migration, 9/11 further transgressed colonial boundaries between the West and the rest, threatening the universality of whiteness as the measure of humanity, producing a white paranoid subjectivity and mode of governmentality that allows exclusion, incarceration, and death to become a state of normality, sustaining "the regime of liberal white life as the norm in Europe, as well as across the wider world" (Sharma, 2009, p. 127). Sharma and Sharma (2003) contend that, in a contemporary epoch of multiculturalism – the 'cultural front' of the 'war on terror' (Sharma, 2009) – where the universal is emptied of significance, whiteness becomes an absent presence that seeks to stand for and be a measure of all humanity, filling the void in order to uphold its own authority. This places demands on non-white immigrants to identify with whiteness; if one doesn't know their "proper place," they become an intimate stranger who is "white but not quite" (p. 7). It is this "dis-Orientation" that induces paranoia; a desire-to-know, to control, entangles with a fear-of-regressing. The increasing circulation of paranoia within the 'war on terror' thus becomes, as Sharma and Sharma (2003) describe, a "contemporary politics (pathology) of a self-fashioning Whiteness" (p. 3) directly related to the West's increasing geopolitical precarity.

As described in Chapter 1, Andrea Smith (2012) describes contemporary US white supremacy as built on three distinct yet intersecting logics, or "pillars": *slaveability,* which anchors capitalism; *genocide,* which anchors colonialism, and *orientalism,* which anchors war. The first, slaveability, depends on a racial hierarchy to justify the making of one as the property of another, taking the profits of labor. The second, genocide, depends on the disappearance of Indigenous peoples to justify the taking of native land and resources. The third, orientalism, depends on the marking of peoples or nations as both inferior and threatening to justify force in the name of protection. The above theories suggest that when these buried dynamics come close to the surface, cracking it – such as what is currently happening in the US and elsewhere through black, Indigenous, and immigrant justice movements – they trigger paranoia, threatening to expose white violence (Butler, 1993), the perverse role of colonization (Hage, 2003), and the non-universality of whiteness (Sharma & Sharma, 2003), respectively. Paranoia happens when knowing is taken to these fear-full, forbidden places, challenging white ignorance, enflaming a fear-of-regressing, making the pillars of white supremacy wobble. White supremacy creates the affective conditions for its own dis-ease.

Psycurity

As mentioned above, assemblages are animated by desire.[5] In this section I argue that, with regard to the prodrome machine, these coils are made up of paranoia – a desire-to-know entangled with a fear-of-regressing. And, further, that this unsettling potential is trafficked through *psycurity*. Psycurity is a term I offer for a contemporary 'abstract machine' that directs assemblages to channel paranoia in ways that animate a neocolonial security state. A kind of virtual double to their material counterparts (Patton, 2000), an abstract machine is a sociopolitical blueprint that operates, "like a little refrain, a tune that gains its consistency through being repeated over and over again" (Goodchild, 1996, p. 50). Here, this little refrain has taken an overcoding state, reterritorializing paranoia into not only prodromal production but also white supremacy. Within psycurity, paranoia does not make the pillars of white supremacy wobble; it curls around them, seeping into the cracks, stabilizing it.

As introduced in Chapters 2 and 3, the prodrome machine works as a checkpoint within a control society – a serpent that modulates bodies in ways that are "undulatory, in orbit, a continuous network" (p. 6). As a psycurity assemblage, this expression is animated by paranoia, thus suggesting that paranoia moves with a similar undulation. In what follows, then, I consider these serpentine movements by thinking with the prodrome machine.

Hiding

First, desire-to-know appears to move through psycurity assemblages as rational. This can be seen in the prodrome machine whereby the cogs are presented as objective, stuck together with trust in the authority of Science, methodically probing and cataloging the world – as Fanon (1952) describes colonial rationality. However, this desire-to-know entangles with a fear-of-regressing because of its proximity to the *ir*rational – namely, with regard to the prodrome machine, the madness that it is enclosing.

As mentioned above, Butler (1993) describes how paranoia is triggered by the potential of some distance being crossed, endangering the virgin sanctity of whatever feels threatened. In the prodrome machine this is conceivably Science itself. Nearby, prodromal experiences question what is assumed to be rational; a proximity to irrationality that perhaps leads to increased claims of objectivity. As Maldonado-Torres (2016) writes, cries of and for "'objectivity,' and other lofty ideals such as excellence, are used to keep or increase the boundaries between those who claim to be in the zone of being human and those condemned to the zone of . . . dehumanization" (p. 14). However, this distance is dependent on the descent of current-day classifications of psychosis from the same nineteenth century erection of boundaries around 'reason' that separated 'man' from 'woman,' 'adult' from 'child,' and 'the civilized' from 'the primitive' (Blackman, 2001); the making of one as reason-able is dependent on another as un-reason-able. It follows that paranoia-as-Science may, in fact, rely on paranoia-as-symptom.

Thus that paranoia moves within psycurity may enact how, within coloniality, the standards of reason constantly change (Fanon, 1952). This slipperiness takes a distinct shape in contemporary conditions. For Hook (2012), "subtle shifts in cardinal anxieties and perceived societal lacks will be reflected in what is most angering, most menacing in today's other" (p. 145); it seems plausible that the post-9/11 accelerated attention to the prodrome, a figure of potentially pathological paranoia, may be reflecting the irrationality of the current US politics of terror. This suggestion perhaps also offers explanation to the ferocity with which 'we' seem to have grabbed on, and clung, to discourses of paranoia as a symptom of an inherited, diseased entity: the Psychotic Disorder. It is a remarkably effective strategy for keeping Those who are surveilled distinct from Us who are surveilling, and thus our own madness distinct from Us, too. Indeed, Harper (2008) describes how paranoid people become a 'serviceable other' that not only allow the construction of ourselves as "trusting; rational; reasonable; optimistic; sane and so on" but enable the continued circulation of a suspicion that reinforces a security state (p. 21; see also Rose, 2010; Seddon, 2010). With regard to the prodrome machine, this suggests that scientific operations may abet these dynamics, enabling paranoia to once again posture as if it were an unmarked frame, laying claim to the authority of a direct perception (Butler, 1993). Thus, a rational desire-to-know enflames a fear-of-regressing to irrationality leads to a rational desire-to-know . . . This looping enables paranoia to spiral away from unreasonable suspicion. Psycurity may direct paranoia to hide as reasonable suspicion.

Predicting

Second, desire-to-know appears to move through psycurity as controlling. This can be seen in the prodrome machine as its early warning signs, pre-screening questionnaires, and evaluations are all deployed to identify prodromes that can then be used to collect risk factors, create algorithms, and calculate potential psychosis – as stuck together with an urgency that this threat is looming. However, this desire-to-know entangles with a fear-of-regressing because the data produced is testimony to an *un*controllability – as described in Chapter 2, the prodromal movement is struggling to make its predictions.

Brian Massumi (2010) argues that pre-emptive logic is based on a double conditional – the 'would-have/could-have.' Present threat, he explains, is a "step by step regress from the certainty of actual fact" (p. 55). The 'actual fact' would be that one *is* psychotic; one step back is that one *has the capacity for* psychosis; another step back is that one does not have the capacity but *would have if they could have*. This 'would have' is grounded in the assumption that a prodromal diagnosis signifies the presence of a chronic pathological entity; the 'could have' is grounded in the assumption that pre-emptive treatment is actually blocking one's future psychosis. Such a double conditional can be seen in explanations for an overall decline in the proportion of prodromes that become psychotic in prodromal studies. Researchers write that this is from effective prodromal treatments, earlier detections leading to later onsets, and a 'dilution effect' from an increase in people who are "not really at risk being referred to HR [high risk] services, possibly as a result of these services and their intake criteria becoming more well-known" (Fusar-Poli, 2013, n.p.). They would have become psychotic, if they could have. Any lack of capacity to calculate is interpreted as the success of the movement, rather than as challenging its founding assumption: that psychosis is predictable. The prodrome machine suggests that, within psycurity, increasing evidence of uncontrollability leads to increased attempts to calculate it.

And yet, what is being controlled in this assemblage is a potential. In particular, it is *threat* – what Massumi (2005) understands as the primary object of governance in post-9/11 US. Threat is a virtual future that triggers material interventions in the present, such as the dissemination of early warning signs that act as signs of alert that the threat is not just near, but here. In turn, psycurity assemblages work as a 'quasi-causal operation' whereby interventions in the present become predictions of the future. Here, what is yet to occur takes "blaring precedence over what has actually happened" (p. 52); a "non-existent entity" has "come from the future to fill the present with menace" (p. 52). Moreover, as mentioned in Chapter 2, pre-emptive interventions disable the falsification of these predictions. Prodromal treatments, for example, enter people into an "open-ended" threat whereby their riskiness "will have been real for all eternity" (p. 53). In this way, psychosis becomes an "unconsummated surplus of danger" (p. 53) – there is always the potential that it might appear even if there has been no clear and present evidence of such. It is this "nagging" that gives threat its capacity for self-renewal. Through the prodrome machine, one's future menace – psychosis – is "once and for all in the non-linear time of its own causing" (p. 53).

Thus, a controlling desire-to-know enflames a fear-of-regressing to being out of control leads to a controlling desire-to-know . . . This looping enables paranoia to make its own object. Psycurity may direct paranoia to predict the future.

Branding

Third, desire-to-know appears to move through psycurity as othering. We can see this in the prodrome machine whereby education-*cum*-recruitment strategies, stuck together with compassion, are used to produce a market of prodromes. However, this desire-to-know entangles with a fear-of-regressing because this marketing suggests that the other may not exist, indeed that the pathologizing gaze is perhaps better turned towards the movement itself.

Within control societies, our everyday movements have become a value-producing labor, or what Deleuze and Guattari (1972) call a 'surplus value of flow,' feeding our trace back to corporations that can then use it to capture a bigger market. With regard to the prodrome machine, this corporation is 'the movement' – that amorphous transnational program of research made up of numerous, shifting sites of studies and stakeholders – be they government officials, psychiatric professionals, clinical researchers, school and community members, family members, or prodromes themselves. The everyday motions of the prodrome produce a surplus value through their pathological excesses – those parts of their experiences, lives, and flesh that linger too close to psychosis. These biological differences then become produced as 'risk factors' that circulate and generate capital (Clough & Willse, 2010) – making populations for research funding, authority for prodromal professions, consumers for drug companies, persuasion for political campaigns, and decoys for gun lobbies. Stationed at borders (rather than institutions), prodromal researchers have the task of safeguarding these flows, ensuring their continuation.

For Deleuze (1992), marketing is the 'soul' of these corporations. Indeed NAPLS, who since their beginnings have proudly described themselves as a 'self-governing enterprise' (Addington et al., 2007), explicitly use the term "marketing" to describe their recruitment strategies (e.g., Addington et al., 2012). Moreover, as mentioned in Chapter 2, in 2015 they enthusiastically supported the roll out of a campaign across eight towns in Connecticut that, while officially to reduce the amount of "untreated psychosis" in young people, was also expected to capture potential prodromes for the local prodromal research clinic. Couched in terms of "public education," their specific tactics were designed to "employ novel social marketing approaches" including,

> ...[the] development of a campaign brand image and logo, the use of analytic tools (e.g. Google analytics) to assess online traffic related to STEP-ED's message disaggregated by target sub-populations (e.g. age, gender, town of residence) with the ability to course correct the targeting of messages.
> *(Srihari et al., 2014, n.p.)*

This slippage between education and recruitment *and* marketing shows that the prodrome machine is not just feeding itself with its own regurgitated risk factors but also convincing people to invest their own or an other's body into it, thereby selling itself too. As enacted through the imposition of quotas in Chapter 3, this marketing is driven by a demand for numbers and thus statistical power. As is typical of a molar assemblage, the prodrome machine increases its power in a linear, quantitative fashion through the incorporation of new bodies. Yet, as stated by NAPLS regarding the launch of their program of their study, these bodies are not only "hard to find," they are rare (Addington et al., 2007, n.p.). The fleeting existence of the other leads to increased marketing.

However, the marketing of the prodrome machine involves more than branding the campaign image and logo referred to above. It is also enacting a 'political branding' – using data to stamp historically threatening bodies, entangling racism with statistical populations (Clough & Willse, 2010). This seems particularly pertinent for the prodrome machine given that – as mentioned in Chapter 2 – psychosis has come to land disproportionately in black bodies after the diagnosis came to pathologize anti-racist activists during the US black resistance movements of the sixties and seventies (Metzl, 2009).

Arguably, this pathologizing was not simply because these bodies were black; it was because they threatened white supremacy. A threat that can also be attributed to mass shootings by white men. As discussed in Chapter 2, to attribute these killings to mental illness is to avoid a pathologizing gaze at the culture and nation that produces them, thus enabling a post-9/11 milieu that demands a clear distinction between 'domestic shooters' and 'foreign terrorists' in order to maintain not only US white supremacy but American exceptionalism.

Thus, an othering desire-to-know enflames a fear-of-regressing to the other leads to an othering desire-to-know . . . This looping enables paranoia to do racism. Psycurity may direct paranoia to brand threatening bodies.

Growing

With their eternal loopiness, hiding, predicting and branding give paranoia momentum. However, because these coils all involve fear – of the irrational, the uncontrollable, and the other within – they also make paranoia grow. This circulation of fear is most evident within the prodrome machine with the invoking of the Sandy Hook shooting – keeping the fear of the irrational, the uncontrollable, and the other within nearby, stirring a rational, controlling, othering desire-to-know. However, as described in Chapter 2, it is also operating within a post-9/11 context governed by fear. Massumi (2010) writes of how, within this context, a 'political ontology' of threat is created by not only the productive power of pre-emption mentioned above, but also the 'affective fact' of fear, whereby "the non-existence of what has not happened be[comes] *more* real than what is now observably over and done with" (p. 52). This affect-driven logic "saves threat from having to materialize as a clear and present danger – or even an emergent danger – in order to command action" (p. 55). Thus it is perhaps its operation on this affective register that, at least in part, enables the prodrome machine to build despite its slippery reasoning, incapacity to predict, and lack of prodromal bodies. Joining with the fear-full context of Sandy Hook and post-9/11, one's potential psychosis becomes an affective fact in the present. In turn, the prodrome machine "grows like a crystal in hypersaturated solution" (p. 130) – to borrow Eve Sedgwick's (2003) description of paranoia.

Thus, a rational, controlling, othering desire-to-know enflames a fear-of-regressing to the irrational, the uncontrollable, and the other within leads to a rational, controlling, othering desire-to-know . . . This looping swells within a political context hypersaturated with terror. Psycurity may direct paranoia to grow through fear, turning its loops into spirals.

Supremacy

The above image suggests that, as a checkpoint within a control society, the prodrome machine is driven by a psycurity that directs paranoia to hide as reasonable suspicion, predict the future, brand threatening bodies, and grow through fear. In turn, these coils of paranoia offer to lubricate the seven figures put forth by Chela Sandoval (2000; in dialogue with Roland Barthes) as sustaining white supremacy. Driving objectivity, paranoia's hiding enables both a 'privation of history' and 'neither-norism' – distancing the prodromal movement from its own story, making it 'happy but ignorant,' and presenting a neutrality that enacts a detached, non-extreme way of being. Driving calculation, paranoia's predicting enables both a 'statement of fact' and 'quantification' – speaking and knowing with certainty, asserting reality as if there were no other, and turning one's future into formula. Driving marketing, paranoia's branding enables both an 'identification' and 'inoculation' – consuming madness as a universal biological aberration that can be folded into whiteness without threatening it, and treating difference as a controlled substance, injecting it homeopathically, leading to tolerance while taming and domesticating anything that might otherwise interrupt a supremacist society. And, growing through a fear that both obliges and emerges from perpetual pre-emption, these paranoid coils together enable a spiraling 'tautology' – trapping us inside a psycuritized episteme.

For Sandoval (2000), these naturalized and seemingly harmless figures ultimately work to erase difference, thus contributing to the ongoing 'metaphysical catastrophe' of colonization by, as Maldonado-Torres (2016) describes, creating "a global community with similar priorities, perceptions, and desires" (p. 13). Perhaps, then, this is how psycurity ultimately animates a neocolonial security state; directing paranoia to hide, predict, brand, and grow such that it erases difference. As suggested above, white supremacy creates the affective conditions for its own dis-ease: paranoia happens when knowing is taken to fear-full, forbidden places – places that suggest possibilities outside of the ignorant colonial episteme, places of difference, of other worlds. Sensing cracks in its pillars, paranoia makes white supremacy wobble. However, if psycurity can direct paranoia to erase difference, it can fill – not expose – any such cracks, thereby animating – not unsettling – a neocolonial security state.

Further, the above mapping of the prodrome machine is not necessarily *the* image of psycurity. Psycurity assemblages perhaps come in a number of different forms. For example, since the 1990s the New York City Police Department (NYPD) has deployed 'quality of life' policing that criminalizes non-criminal behavior in the name of crime prevention, rationalizing a statistical and physical stalking of bodies that are considered at risk of becoming criminal. One of these practices is 'stop and frisk,' whereby police stop and question any person whom they reasonably suspect has committed, is currently committing, or is about to commit a crime, and then frisk them if they think they are carrying a weapon. Between January 2004 and June 2012, the NYPD conducted over 4.4 million such stops – the vast majority of which involved young black men, suggesting that the NYPD use "race as a proxy for crime" (Zamani, 2015, p. 2). This racism emerges in a criminal justice system that has a history of protecting white supremacy and that imposes quotas as a measure of officer accountability – together creating the conditions of possibility for the over-policing of black communities (Alexander, 2010; Browne-Marshall, 2013). This context sheds light on why 'furtive behavior' is the most common reason given by the NYPD for making these stops; far from a sign of one's potential criminality, people are suspecting imminent police brutality. 'Quality of life' policing is thus perhaps also an expression of psycurity that – itself oscillating between quotas and calculators – hides paranoia as 'reasonable suspicion,' distinguishing it from the furtiveness of its suspicious objects and directing it to predict criminals, brand black bodies, and grow in a post-9/11 hypersaturated solution of fear of blackness, of those who revolt against white supremacy, who know that Black Lives Matter[6].

As another possible example: after 9/11, the NYPD also established a secret surveillance program that mapped, monitored, and analyzed Muslim daily life throughout New York City and its surrounding states. NYPD informants and undercover agents infiltrated 'hot spots' such as religious spaces and popular cafes, creating what Diala Shamas and Nermeen Arastu (2015) describe as a pervasive "atmosphere of tension, mistrust and suspicion" in Muslim communities (p. 4). In particular, these authors note a silencing of conversations and actions relating to foreign policy and civil rights – including "a qualitative shift in the way individuals joke, the types of metaphors they use, and even the sort of coffee house chatter in which they engage" (p. 4) – as well as a distrust toward both each other and local police. And yet, proponents of the surveillance argue that, "mere spying on a community is harmless because it is clandestine and that those who are targeted should have nothing to fear, if they have nothing to hide" (p. 4). Muslim people's suspicion makes them suspicious; the 'reasonable suspicion' of the NYPD is differentiated from the unreasonable suspicion that they both create and criminalize. Muslim surveillance is thus perhaps also an expression of psycurity – directing paranoia to hide, predict terrorists, brand bodies of North African, Middle Eastern, and South Asian descent[7], and grow in a post-9/11 hypersaturated solution of Islamophobia and 'terror.'

Seeping into the cracks of white supremacy, these paranoid coils are suffocating. And yet, psycurity assemblages may be even more shifty. Sedgwick (2003) writes how the 'hermeneutics of suspicion' with which critical scholars are trained have had an "unintentionally stultifying side effect" (p. 124): the privileging of paranoia. This,

> has by now candidly become less a diagnosis than a prescription. In a world where no one need be delusional to find evidence of systemic oppression, to theorize out of anything but a paranoid critical stance has come to seem naïve, pious, or complaisant.
>
> *(p. 125)*

Driven by paranoia, critical scholarship – including critical psychology – may itself express psycurity. However, Sedgwick asks if criticality has to be paranoid, arguing that it can perhaps be reparative too. Moreover, Michel Foucault (1983) argues that the concept of assemblage offers a number of principles for "the art of living *counter* to all forms of fascism" (p. xiii, my emphasis). The first of these principles is, "Free political action from all unifying and totalizing paranoia" (p. xiii). Albeit explicitly witnessing paranoia's stifling effects, Foucault's adjectives imply that there may be more than one kind of paranoia, one that is neither unifying nor totalizing. And, further, that this potential may come from psycurity assemblages themselves. Thus, given that psycurity assemblages are checkpoints within a control society, a serpent, in the next chapter I stage an encounter between the prodrome and Coatlicue, a Mesoamerican goddess of the serpent as introduced by Anzaldúa (1987), for guidance on reparative potentials within the paranoid coils of a neocolonial security state.

Notes

1. Hamid Dabashi (2015) wonders if Frantz Fanon risks becoming a "frozen talisman for Europeans to cite to prove they are not philosophically racist" (n.p.).
2. 'Make America Great Again' was the slogan for Donald Trump's presidential campaign, inciting an emphatic and recurring response from activists that 'America' was never great for people that did not conform to the raced and gendered status quo. While Stephen Frosh (2016) does not specify which context he is writing from and to, his analysis inadvertently echoes with this rhetoric and is thus useful for thinking through the wily nature of whiteness.
3. Rodney King was a black man who was brutally beaten by a group of white Los Angeles Police Department officers in March 1991. The beating was caught on videotape; however, a mostly white jury acquitted the officers in 1992, triggering five days of widespread protest known as the 'LA riots.'
4. We can see this in the manifesto of Dylann Roof, whose racist rage was triggered when, in response to the shooting of Travon Martin, he typed "black on

White crime" into Google. Demonizing black people and positioning themselves as victims is a common tactic of white nationalist groups, who use the idea of black-on-white-crime as a justification for needing their own state (SPLC, 2015).

5 For Isabelle Stengers (2012), thinking through and with assemblages may help to heal the abovementioned colonial divide between Knower and Known, Truth and Illusion, as it offers something aside from binaries to conceptualize reality. Chela Sandoval (2000) too names this Deleuzian philosophy as one that defies and remakes Western thought and organization – aligning it with decolonizing scholars including Gloria Anzaldúa and Aime Césaire. Within this kind of image, agency does not lie with an 'I,' it belongs to assemblages as desire, or what Stengers (2012) calls 'animation.' As Paul Patton (2000) writes, "Desire is present in a given assemblage in the same way that, in a musical work, the principle of composition is present in the silences as much as in the audible sounds" (p. 70). It follows that desire is implicated in all social and political processes, that all relations are desire relations. This desire is positive, productive, and constructivist: it is a primary active force, it makes things happen between bodies, and it requires an assemblage. Thus, rather than being an entity of some sort, Deleuzian desire is more accurately a process of production that connects and encodes various elements of an assemblage, making intensities from which experiences are derived. Desire is therefore a creative force. In turn, assemblages can be read in terms of how they channel this potential.

6 'Black Lives Matter' is used to refer to anti-racist activism that has grown in resistance to recent police killings of black communities in the US. It stands on the shoulders of centuries of struggle against this and other forms of white supremacy and incited the creation of the Movement for Black Lives – a coalition of black-led organizations working for black liberation.

7 I write this not as an exhaustive list of all Muslim bodies, but in reference to those who are most likely to be read as 'Muslim'.

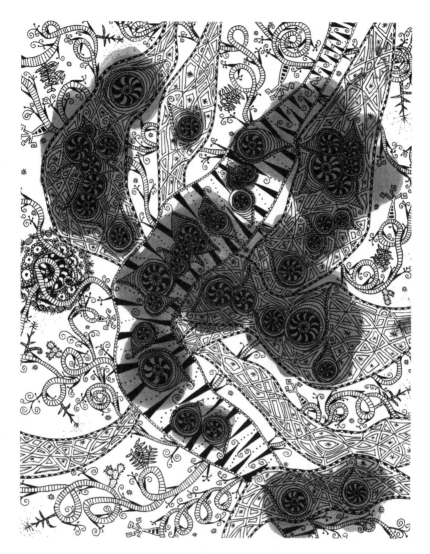

DRAWING 4. "Bleeding." Black ink on cochineal print, el Jardín Etnobotánico de Oaxaca. Rachel Jane Liebert, 2016.

5
ROOTS[1]

While in the previous chapter I consider how, driven by its own paranoia, the prodromal movement enacts a neocolonial security state, here I wonder if there might be more to this psycurity assemblage than met my critical psychological eye. Eve Sedgwick (2003) sees paranoia as a relational stance that works to anticipate, generalize, and expose in order to avoid surprises and humiliation, and thus the affective drive of scholarship that seeks to do the same; what she calls a *paranoid reading*. Yet, "for someone to have an unmystified view of systemic oppressions does not *intrinsically* or *necessarily* enjoin that person to any specific train of epistemological or narrative consequences" (p. 127, her emphasis). Indeed, as depicted in the coils of Chapter 4, paranoia has a mode of selective scanning and a mushrooming, self-confirming strength that may "circumscribes its potential as a medium of political or cultural struggle" (p. 130). Sedgwick thus calls for paranoid readings to not be seen as mandatory so much as one of many possible ways of being 'critical.' Resonating with decolonizing warnings about an epistemic violence that strips away diversity and agency (e.g., Mohanty, 2003; Spivak, 1988), her analysis reshapes a response-ability for Psychology in the present political moment. As opposed to the 'strong theory' of paranoid readings, so weighty it can't be moved, she suggests experimenting with 'weak theory,' with making multiple, localized, unstable knowledges that – welcoming surprise and organized with hope – do justice to a wider affective range.

Below I re-enter the prodromal movement to experiment with this kind of *reparative reading* of paranoia itself, looking for a 'space of disjunct' within the fearful coils of psycurity (McManus, 2011). In Chapter 3 I considered how the prodromal movement mobilizes against the infernal alternative that people's experiences are Normal, protecting both itself and 'America.' For Philippe Pignarre and Isabelle Stengers (2011), this defensive dynamic "mesmerize[s] thinking" (p. 30) – what they come to describe as a kind of *sorcery*. To be bewitched is to have learned to "scorn the questions that a 'true' scientist shouldn't pose" (p. 32). Inspired by a desire-to-know beside paranoia, I shall attempt to ask one of these questions. And to do so, I also invoke the otherworldly, meeting witchcraft with witchcraft.

Wound

> Come, little green snake. Let the wound caused by the serpent be cured by the serpent.
>
> *(Anzaldúa, 1987, p. 68)*

Paranoia can perhaps be conceived as what Lisa Blackman (2012) calls 'threshold phenomena,' or that which implies "some kind of transport between the self and other, inside and outside, and material and immaterial" (p. 20). Drawing on Karen Barad (2007), by 'phenomenon' Blackman (2010) signals that these experiences are not pre-existing entities, discoverable through measurement, so much as emerging through the intra-action of a variety of entangled agencies. This relational ontology allows symptoms of psychosis such as voice-hearing, telepathy, and (perhaps, as I attempt to sketch) paranoia, to destabilize the typical subject of Psychology, opening up a more "trans-subjective sense of the psychic or psychological as a shared, collective encounter or event" (p. 11–12). When taking this trans-subjective stance, however, Blackman (2014) rejects temptations to designate it as in some way 'new.' For such not only assumes a shift from one episteme to another, thereby "reproducing the very progressivist and linear narratives that have been reworked over and over in our critical thinking" (p. 2), but ignores the continuation of *dis*continuities, of that which is "transmitted through silences, gaps, omissions, echoes, and murmurs" (p. 2).

In turn, Blackman (2010, 2012, 2014) tunes into nineteenth-century tales of Western psychological experimentation to hear from threshold phenomena. I have also been called by discontinuities, however my listening has taken a different direction; one that is in part inspired by Steve Brown and Paul Stenner's (2009) introduction to their influential book, *Psychology Without Foundations*. Dedicated to rethinking models of subjectivity in Psychology through an assembling of alternative theoretical resources,

Brown and Stenner use the tale of *Moby Dick* to push Psychology away from taking an 'Ahab-function' that aims to "find and have done with the whale" and toward an 'Ishmael-function' that aims instead to "follow the whale, wherever it takes us, endlessly" (p. 5). The 'whale,' in this case, being the psyche; one that is otherwise hunted, captured, killed by Western psychological trappings. To prepare for this Ishmael-function, Brown and Stenner draw on six "key thinkers"; a tactic that comes with a somewhat surprising acknowledgment:

> We are uncomfortably aware of the fact that our thinkers are all white, European males . . . This selection rather obviously reflects our peculiar intellectual paths and our particular interests and desires. Equally obviously it should not be taken as suggesting that these are the only thinkers worth engaging with . . .
>
> *(pp. 6–7)*

In her phenomenology of whiteness, Sara Ahmed (2007) documents how discomfort signals a usual comfort, of being "so at ease with one's environment that it is hard to distinguish where one's body ends and the world begins" (p. 158). This environment is one that is 'white' – ready for certain kinds of bodies, perpetually shaped by their habits, and inherited from colonization; Brown and Stenner's (2009) discomfort echoes with another connection between Psychology and whaling. Pursuing not just any whale but a prized white one embroiled in the currents of nineteenth-century capitalist expansion, *Moby Dick* isn't simply "an exemplary demonstration of *human* endeavour" (p. 1, my emphasis), it is a colonial one.

Within this context, the above intellectual path does not seem so peculiar, nor does it seem so obvious that non-white, non-European, non-male thinkers are worthy of engagement. Especially given that predominantly thinking with white, European males appears to remain the norm if not the demand when turning to affect – despite over a decade of critique of these knowledge practices for doing so (e.g., Hemmings, 2005). Not only does this prolong an erroneous sense of newness within such scholarship (Tuck & McKenzie, 2015; Todd, 2016), it both presumes and erases settler colonial epistemologies, "unwittingly reifying the normatively White Enlightenment subject, and the settler colonial grounds on which it is formed" (Rowe & Tuck, 2016, p. 5). To habitually cite the thought of white, European males contributes to the epistemologies of ignorance (Alcoff, 2007) haunting both Psychology and studies of affect – productions that, as discussed in Chapter 4, have been crucial to the ascent of whiteness (Mills, 2007). Brown and Stenner's (2009) discomfort, then, offers a generous, generative site for those of us who, like them, yearn for a more responsive Psychology in the present political moment. Thus, in a continued experiment with the 'border thinking' introduced in Chapter 1 (Mignolo, 2012), below I see what happens if the familiar interlocutor of Psychology is put into conversation with the unfamiliar. Etymologically joining *para* (beside) with *nous* (mind), 'paranoia' denotes an experience *beside-the-mind*. I follow these roots to meet their more-than-human figure (Miller, 1977), as introduced through Chicana philosopher and poet, Gloria Anzaldúa (1987) – seeing if a cause of our political and scholarly wounds might also be a cure.

Cliff

> If you can tell me all on your own that it's not real, it's a four. If I need to throw you a line that it might be a part of your imagination, it's a five.

I jotted down this quote in 2014, when I was sitting around a table with seven other people in the same very small, very hot, very bare room that I introduced in Chapter 3, participating in a training session to learn how to use the Structured Interview for Psychosis-Risk Syndromes (SIPS; as introduced in Chapter 2). Usually two days long, I was invited to this one-off one-day event after it was pulled together by special request for three participants from Santiago who had been funded by the Chilean government to establish the first prodromal clinic in their country. They bought a gift (chocolate, I think), thrilled for the opportunity to be trained by our trainer – the Research Clinical Coordinator (RCC) part of the North American Prodromal Longitudinal Study (NAPLS) that I introduced in Chapter 2.

Over seven hours of rapid-fire training we were shown how the SIPS – woven together with nearly 40 pages of questions – throws its think-net over 'unusual thought content,' 'suspiciousness,' 'grandiose ideas,' 'perceptual abnormalities' and 'disorganized communication.' Collectively called 'attenuated psychotic symptoms,' these experiences are illustrated by its inventors, Tandy Miller and colleagues (1999), with the following:

> Patients experiencing such symptoms can report hearing odd noises, such as banging or clicking or ringing; dogs barking when there is no animal present; or their name being called when no one has called them. More severe but still attenuated symptoms have been described as hearing sounds or voices that seem far away or mumbled. People also report experiencing vague perceptual changes such as seeing colors

differently, seeing flashes of light, or seeing geometric shapes. People have also frequently reported seeing shadows out of the corner of their eyes or vague ghostlike figures.

(p. 706)

The SIPS extracts these kind of experiences with a battery of yes/no questions and allocates a rating between zero and six – zero meaning the symptom is "absent," six meaning it is "floridly psychotic," and three, four, or five meaning that it is "at-risk," that the young person experiencing it is prodromal. During the training we were offered a "cheat sheet" to differentiate between these seven scores. While in Chapter 3 I describe the borderguards that patrol the border between Prodromal and Normal, blocking the movement's infernal alternative, another border was also present – that between five and six, the gate between Prodromal and Psychotic. This rating hinged "most importantly" on whether or not someone could "self-disclose their doubt." If they could not – if you "let people talk and talk and talk" about their experience and they "never say it's not real" – then they cross the border into madness.

Except that we were taught another, unofficial, "trick." Conceptualizing an individual as at this point "hanging over a cliff," RCC directed us to "throw them a line" by asking a question: *"Did you ever consider the possibility that this was part of your imagination?"* If the young person "grabs the line" – saying "Yes" to this question – we are to give them a five; if they don't grab the line – saying "No, it was real" or "It felt real" – we are to give them a six, watching as they tumble over the edge into Psychotic Disorder. Curled through with what Alfred North Whitehead (1920) named the "bifurcation of nature," this trick presumes that perception is divided into two sets of things, effectively: 'nature' + 'psychic additions':

> For example, what is given in perception is the green grass. This is an object which we know as an ingredient in nature. The theory of psychic additions would treat the greenness as a psychic addition furnished by the perceiving mind, and would leave to nature merely the molecules and the radiant energy which influence the mind towards that perception.
>
> (p. 29)

The SIPS, then, patrols for those psychic additions gone awry. It is the descendant of an influential manual of perceptual disturbances in college students who were "probably at high-risk for psychosis" as per their responses to true/false scales said to identify "traits of the schizophrenia prone" (Chapman & Chapman, 1980, p. 48). One such scale was Perceptual Aberration

(Chapman et al., 1978), based on a psychoanalytic conceptualization of Schizophrenia as ultimately being disturbances in one's ability to establish and maintain boundaries – particularly those relating to the body (e.g., Item 1: "Sometimes I have had the feeling that I am united with an object near me"). Through a series of interviews with these students, Loren Chapman and Jean Chapman (1980) organized 80 types of "deviant" experiences into six categories of symptoms, becoming the first to put forth an argument for, and manual of, "attenuated psychosis." Large disclaimer included:

> We believe that the rating values given in this scale are suitable for most white persons from the United States and the general Western cultural tradition. We do not know if these values are suitable for blacks or for members of other minority subcultures.
>
> *(p. 479)*

This concession of cross-cultural *in*validity has carried through the prodromal field. The same research group went on to develop a series of individual scales based on this manual to identify "psychosis-prone" young adults. One such scale is Magical Ideation (e.g., Item 19: "I have sometimes sensed an evil presence around me, although I could not see it"), or the "belief, quasi-belief, or semi-serious entertainment of the possibility that events which, according to the causal concepts of *this* culture, cannot have a causal relation with each other, might somehow nevertheless do so" (Meehl, 1964, p. 54, as cited in Eckblad and Chapman, 1983, my emphasis). Left unnamed, the "this" of this definition floats quietly by, at once ignoring and incising a familiar standard: "the general Western cultural tradition." As with their previous work, these authors emphasize that it is not *what* people experience so much as *how* they interpret them that determines psychosis. What matters is their degree of conviction that something 'really' happened. The idea that people might accurately be sensing these seemingly impossible bodily and causal relations appears to not even warrant a passing thought.

The SIPS has inherited a legacy that separates the act of perceiving from that which is perceived, enabling the former to be assessed, judged, fixed. Whitehead ultimately responds to this bifurcation of nature by invoking his own "strange God" (Latour, 2011; Stengers, 2011); in what follows I likewise respond. But by thinking with a different strange god(dess).

Coatlicue[2]

It is her reluctance to cross over, to make a hole on the fence and walk across, to cross the river, to take that flying leap into the dark, that drives her to escape, that forces her into the fecund cave of her imagination where she is cradled in the arms of Coatlicue, who will never let her go. If she doesn't change her ways, she will remain a stone forever. No hay mas que cambiar.

(Anzaldúa, 1987, p. 71)

Here, Anzaldúa (1987) invokes Coatlicue, the earliest of the Mexica fertility and Earth goddesses. Known also as the Lady of the Serpent Skirt, 'Coatlicue' comes from *coatl*, the Nahuatl word for serpent, the most significant symbol for pre-colonial America, associated with the womb "from which all things were born and to which all things returned" (p. 56). Indeed, with *coatl* also meaning twin, Coatlicue represents duality, its synthesis, and something more:

After each of my four bouts with death I'd catch glimpses of an otherworld Serpent. Once, in my bedroom, I saw a cobra the size of the room, her hood expanding over me. When I blinked she was gone. I realized she was, in my psyche, the mental picture and symbol of the instinctual in its collective impersonal, pre-human. She, the symbol of the dark sexual drive, the chthonic (underworld), the feminine, the serpentine movement of sexuality, of creativity, the basis of all energy and life.

(p. 57)

For Anzaldúa, this "instinctual in its collective impersonal, pre-human" is a conflicted desire – a creative "fusion of opposites" (p. 69), an ancient fleshed knowing emerging from a painful assimilation to being animal:

Snakes, viboras: since that day I've sought and shunned them. Always when they cross my path, fear and elation flood my body. I know things older than Freud, older than gender. She – that's how I think of la Vibora, Snake Woman. Like the ancient Olmec, I know Earth is a coiled Serpent. Forty years it's taken me to enter into the Serpent, to acknowledge that I have a body, that I am a body and to assimilate the animal body, the animal soul.

(p. 48)

Containing and balancing the dualities of male and female, light and dark, life and death, Anzaldúa documents how Coatlicue was divided, darkened, and disempowered through colonization. Pushed underground, this burying of "balanced oppositions" fertilized the growth of a militaristic, bureaucratic, predatory state – a description that notably echoes in present-day US, in the neocolonial security state.

And yet to be buried is to be planted. An entrance into the Serpent, into living with Coatlicue, brings forth 'la facultad,' a "capacity to see in surface phenomena the meaning of deeper realities":

> It is an instant "sensing," a quick perception arrived at without conscious reasoning. It is an acute awareness mediated by the part of the psyche that does not speak, that communicates in images and symbols which are the faces of feelings, that is, behind which feelings reside/hide. The one possessing this sensitivity is excruciatingly alive to the world.
>
> *(p. 60)*

"Latent in all of us," la facultad takes shape under pressure and from the margins; more highly tuned within people who do not feel psychologically or physically safe – "the females, the homosexuals of all races, the darkskinned, the outcast, the persecuted, the marginalized, the foreign" (p. 60). A "kind of survival tactic that people, caught between worlds, unknowingly cultivate" (p. 61), la facultad is how one listens to and heeds the world.

> I walk into a house and I know whether it is empty or occupied. I feel the lingering charge in the air of a recent fight or love-making or depression. I sense the emotions someone near is emitting – whether friendly or threatening. Hate and fear – the more intense the emotion, the greater my reception of it. I feel a tingling on my skin when someone is staring at me or thinking about me. I can tell how others feel by the way they smell, where others are by the air pressure on my skin. I can spot the love or greed or generosity lodged in the tissues of another. Often I sense the direction of and my distance from people or objects – in the dark, or with my eyes closed, without looking. It must be a vestige of a proximity sense, a sixth sense that's lain dormant from long-ago times.
>
> *(p. 61)*

I am struck by the resemblance between Anzaldúa's description of la facultad and Miller and colleagues' (1999) description above of attenuated psychotic symptoms, of prodromal experiences thus assumed to be precursors of a pathological paranoia. The former seen as a capacity, the latter as a deficit, their phenomenological overlap points to the ways that Science can 'camp' on examples, staking a territory. For Isabelle Stengers (2011) this is a trap. Empirical projects would better demonstrate 'adequacy' by not invoking anything that will allow an element of experience to be "eliminated, forgotten, treated as an exception or disqualified," and 'applicability' by "demanding that some elements lend themselves to an 'imaginative leap'" by not "communicat[ing] with any normative or even pragmatic privilege" (p. 246). For prodromal research to be a Stengersian success, then, it must be put into conversation with those voices typically not allowed through psycurity, those that one might encounter outside the gates. Coatlicue is one such voice. A leap that involves choosing *not* to grab the line offered by the SIPS, jumping off the cliff and into believing that prodromal experiences are real, flying "far from the solid-ground of evidence" (p. 233), risking a fall into (professional[3]) madness . . .

Borderland

> In attending to this first darkness I am led back to the mystery of the Origin. The one who watches, the one who whispers in a slither of serpents. Something is trying to tell me. That voice at the edge of things. But I know what I want and I stamp ahead, arrogance edging my face. I tremble before the animal, the alien, the sub- or supra-human, the me that has something in common with the wind and the trees and the rocks, that possess a demon determination and ruthlessness beyond human.
>
> *(Anzaldúa, 1987, p. 72)*

Anzaldúa's Coatlicue, "the one who watches, the one who whispers in a slither of serpents," moves through Stengers' (2011) thinking with Whitehead about experience:

> There are other elements in our experience, on the fringe of consciousness, and yet massively qualifying our experience. In regard to these other facts, it is our consciousness that flickers, not the facts themselves. They are always securely there, barely discriminated, and yet inescapable.
>
> *(p. 349)*[4]

Enacting one of Whitehead's ontological principles that "There is nothing which floats into this world from nowhere" (p. 262),[5] these "barely discriminated, and yet inescapable" facts are central to his philosophy of 'prehension' – an underlying activity marking the way that experience participates in the world. Loosely meaning 'taking into account,' a prehensive event can be thought of as a unifying grasp, a gathering of unknown things into a togetherness that can then be known, a "what I will say 'is'" (p. 297). This unification in turn becomes public, available for objectivation, making it "an ingredient for new becomings" (p. 297). Prehension thus makes "the operation and the production of reality coincide" (p. 147). Yet this does not mean that things "owe their reality to that perception" (p. 146). Rather, as Whitehead writes/Stengers cites, prehension "is the perspective of the castle over there from the standpoint of the unification here" (p. 148).[6] Experience, then, is a mode of articulation, testifying to "what is other than it, about other places and other times" (p. 147). It follows that,

> If I feel something, this thing certainly enters into the definition of my experience: it belongs to my experience, and it is not forged by my experience. I sense it insofar as it testifies to something else. I produce myself *qua* feeling that which is not me.
>
> (p. 295)

This articulation does not require a subject or cognitive process – any thing can prehend any thing. Indeed, prehension was coined to exhibit, "the common feature of all situations in which something makes a difference to something else, including the least 'psychological' ones" (p. 147). In doing so Stenger's Whitehead takes experience beyond the human, filling a gap in Psychological thought long taunted by Coatlicue, by Anzaldúa's "me that has something in common with the wind and the trees and the rocks" (p. 72), that unsettles any idea of individuals that are separate from each other and all else that makes up the world. Further, as a process, prehension also witnesses the elements that an actual entity has denied in order to become – a *negative prehension* that is not exclusion so much as "indistinction, or reduction to insignificant noise" (Stengers, 2011, p. 304). That "voice at the edge of things," that flicker. Dormant but not extinct, these whispering potentialities are what Whitehead calls the 'scars' of our feelings:

> A feeling bears on itself the scars of its birth; it recollects as a subjective emotion its struggle for existence; it retains the impress of what it might have been, but is not. It is for this reason that what an actual entity has avoided as a datum for feeling may yet be an important part of its equipment. The actual cannot be reduced to mere matter of fact in divorce from the potential.
>
> (p. 309)[7]

The 'unknown,' then, what could have been, is an important part of 'knowing,' of what is. Whiteheadian philosophy is doing something similar to Anzaldúa, described by Barad (2014) as "pok[ing] a hole in the colonizer's story of how darkness is the other of light, how it sits on the not-light side of the darkness/light binary, about how this story figures darkness as absence, lack, negativity" (p. 171). Symbolizing the fertility of the contradictory, Anzaldúa's (1987) invocation of Coatlicue shows us this potential in the actual, this imagination in the real. In the arms of this strange goddess, the prodrome no longer faces a cliff-edge so much as a borderland:

> Borders are set up to define the places that are safe and unsafe, to distinguish us from them. A border is a dividing line, a narrow strip along a steep edge. A borderland is a vague and undetermined place created by the emotional residue of an unnatural boundary. It is in a constant state of transition. The prohibited and forbidden are its inhabitants.
>
> (p. 25)

Unsettled, unrealized, unwanted, prodrome-the-borderland is first and foremost a space of potential, an emotional residue from negative prehension, wedged between Normal and Psychotic. Patrolling these borders, the SIPS seeks and surveils experiences as they inhabit this in-between space.

Anzaldúa inscribes borderland inhabitants with 'la mestiza consciousness,' a psychic restlessness caused by the coming together of "habitually incompatible frames of reference," creating "a struggle of the flesh, a struggle of borders, an inner war" (p. 100). For Barad (2014), the subsequent underground work, performed by the soul, is a form of diffraction such that, "there is no moving beyond, no leaving the 'old' behind. There is no absolute boundary between here-now and there-then. There is nothing that is new; there is nothing that is not new" (p. 168). As a borderland with no clear dividing lines, just "traces of what might yet (have) happen(ed)" (p. 168), the prodrome is a place where elements are gathering, undetermined as to which will become datum and which will be denied. A hot mess of prehension, it is a lively substrate activity radiating a spectrum of possibilities, where "each bit of matter, each moment of time, each position in space is a multiplicity, a superposition/entanglement of (seemingly) disparate parts" (p. 176).

For Stenger's (2011) Whitehead, such multiplicity is the stuff of cosmology. For Anzaldúa (1987), such cosmology is the stuff of Coatlicue, that "consuming internal whirlwind, the symbol of the underground aspects of the psyche":

> Coatlicue is the mountain, the Earth Mother who conceived all celestial beings out of her cavernous womb. Goddess of birth and death, Coatlicue gives and takes away life; she is the incarnation of cosmic process.
>
> *(p. 68)*

Coatlicue, she who eats the sun and spits out the moon, who makes a circle by eating her own tail, enacts a discontinuous continuity, destroying to create; an eternal possibility emerging from the cracks, alive with those ancient non-known elements of knowing that always have the potential to unite with something else, to make something else, to annihilate something else. Coatlicue, the borderland goddess, stands with la mestiza, the borderland psyche, as she participates in,

> the creation of yet another culture, a new story to explain the world and our participation in it, a new value system with images and symbols that connect us to each other and to the planet. Soy un amasamiento, I am an act of kneading, of uniting and joining that not only has produced both a creature of darkness and a creature of light, but also a creature that questions the definitions of light and dark and gives them new meanings.
>
> *(p. 103)*

Prodrome-the-borderland, then, implies an Anzaldúaian place of alchemical happenings, offering the movement as a site of '(r)evolution' (not revolution; see Chapter 3). In turn this diffracting terrain beckons attention to "its unique material historialities and how they come to matter" (Barad, 2014, p. 176). For Stengers (2011), this mattering depends on the milieu; prehensive events oblige particular ecologies in order for what has been refused to be revealed. With Anzaldúa's Coatlicue and Stenger's Whitehead, the problem of prodromal experiences moves away from the individual and toward the neocolonial security state that they encounter.

Ecology

> Like many Indians and Mexicans, I did not deem my psychic experiences real. I denied their occurrences and let my inner senses atrophy. I allowed white rationality to tell me that the existence of the "other world" was mere pagan superstition. I accepted their reality, the "official" reality of the rational, reasoning mode which is connected with external reality, the upper world, and is considered the most developed consciousness – the consciousness of duality.

The other mode of consciousness facilitates images from the soul and the unconscious through dreams and the imagination. Its work is labeled as "fiction", make-believe, wish-fulfillment. White anthropologists claim that Indians have "primitive" and therefore deficient minds, that we cannot think in the higher mode of consciousness – rationality. They are fascinated by what they call the "magical" mind, the "savage" mind, the *participation mystique* of the mind that says the world of the imagination – the world of the soul – and of the spirit is just as real as physical reality. In trying to become "objective", Western culture made "objects" of things and people when it distanced itself from them, thereby losing "touch" with them. This dichotomy is the root of all violence.

Not only was the brain split into two functions, but so was reality.
(*Anzaldúa, 1987, p. 58–59, her emphasis*)

Here, Anzaldúa writes of a violence moving through 'participation mystique,' a concept first put forth by anthropologist Lucien Levy-Bruhl in his 1910 book, *How Natives Think*. Republished by Princeton University Press in 1985, Levy-Bruhl describes two distinctive elements of 'primitive' – as compared to 'modern' – thinking. First, that it is 'mystical,' that all phenomena are one with each other and thus that human beings are inextricably participating with the world. And second, that it is 'prelogical,' that things are able to simultaneously be both themselves and something else – a thinking that, in his words, "does not bind itself down, as our thought does, to avoiding contradictions" (p. 78). Levy-Bruhl understood this participation mystique to be a consequence of incorrect representations shaping people's conceptions and perceptions of the world and thus *coming between* them and reality, creating outright false beliefs, delusional experiences, and irrationality. In contrast, modern representations were said to shape only people's conceptions and not their perceptions, thereby *conveying* reality. This is because, over time, these representations have supposedly come to filter out an emotionality that otherwise 'colors' thinking, evolving a more rational mind (Segal, 2007).

Robert Segal (2007) documents how Carl Jung used Levy-Bruhl's writing on the participation mystique as data to develop his own ideas about the psyche. While carrying forth the mystical elements, Jung is depicted as leaving behind the prelogical in favor of psychologizing people's experiences. Participation mystique came to be seen as one's unconscious projecting itself onto the world, making us feel (but not really be) connected. This redirection toward the individual lurks in the abovementioned development of the SIPS, based as it is on people having *perceptual* disturbances in their bodily boundaries and causal attributions. Moreover, given that these disturbances are testifying to a wrong psyche *or* a wrong representation (prodromal experiences inside the abovementioned "general Western cultural tradition" suggest potential psychopathology whilst prodromal experiences outside of this context suggest some kind of 'non-Western' cultural belief), the SIPS also sets up a dynamic that maps the contours of modern versus primitive thinking established through the participation mystique. This suggests that the prodromal movement sanctions an enduring colonial encounter; one that positions 'the West' as having come beyond 'the non-West' to directly access the Truth. Indeed, to experience anything other than this is to potentially be psychotic.

Further, such 'primitive thinking' confers a subjectivity to nature that needs to be overcome "in order to dominate her":

> As we know, great minds have wrestled with the problem whether it is the glorious sun that illuminates the world, or the sunlike human eye. Archaic man believes it to be the sun, and civilized man believes it to be the eye . . . He must de-psychize nature in order to dominate her; and in order to see his world objectively he must take back all his archaic projections.
>
> *(Jung, 1931, para. 135)*

Protecting the borders of a manmade world, Jung (1931) writes of how becoming a "great mind" requires that one does not see the world as an extension of their selves. Instead, "Progress comes from seeing the world *as it is*. The external world is really natural rather than supernatural, impersonal rather than personal. Science properly replaces myth and religion as the explanation of the world. There is no turning back" (Segal, 2007, p. 649, my emphasis). As discussed in Chapter 4, Sylvia Wynter (2003) documents how the present-day coloniality of power rests on these sorts of beginnings, which illustrate "the first gradual de-supernaturalizing of our modes of being human" (p. 264); one that required "the systematic stigmatization of the Earth in terms of it being made of a 'vile and base matter,'" "at the center of the universe as its dregs" (p. 367). Indeed, for Trinh Minh-ha (1989), the "supposedly universal tension between Nature and Culture is, in reality, a non-universal hu*man* dis-ease" (p. 67, her emphasis). Any supposed conflict comes from a patriarchal and fearful framing of them as opposite to (rather than different from) one another – exiling the creative potential of matter (Trinh, 1989), preparing the ground for capitalist expansion (Federici, 2014), "no longer playing the game of the world but subjugating it with integers and atoms" (Fanon, 1952, p. 100).

These readings illustrate how those of us of a colonizing lineage, "presume to be the ones who have accepted the hard truth that we are alone in a mute, blind, yet knowable world – one that it is our task to appropriate" (Stengers, 2012,

p. 1). Causing a desire to Know considered in Chapter 4 – a "positivist yearning for transparency with respect to reality" (Trinh, 1989, p. 64) that blocks, refuses, ignores other worlds. A sort of (En)light(ened) pollution that stops us from seeing the stars. This "scientific conquering 'view of the world'" is what Stengers (2012) affiliates with a 'Science' that, "when taken in the singular and with a big *S*, may indeed be described as a general conquest bent on translating everything that exists into objective, rational knowledge" (p. 2). Introduced in Chapter 4, it is this Science that, as Anzaldúa writes above, "made 'objects' of things and people when it distanced itself from them, thereby losing 'touch' with them." Connecting this sort of objectification to the exile of the participation mystique "that says the world of the imagination – the world of the soul – and of the spirit is just as real as physical reality," Anzaldúa's description of how colonization splits reality into two depicts, predicts, politicizes the splitting of imagination and reality – the bifurcating of nature – carried out by the SIPS. Showing us that instruments of psycuritized inquiry perhaps say more about coloniality than the madness we think they are investigating. Indeed, critical psychologists from around the world name the destruction of imagination as central to the colonization of the psyche, such that imagining itself has become a present-day decolonizing praxis (e.g., Segalo, Manoff, & Fine, 2015; Martín-Baro, 1994; Oliver, 2004).

And, the participation mystique suggests that this praxis – imagining – may be about reclaiming an otherworldly correspondence. If so, then this requires "smelling the smoke in our nostrils . . ." (Stengers, 2012, p. 6). Hearing neo-pagan activist, Starhawk, here Stengers is referring here to the smoke coming from the stakes on which witches were burnt, and thus from the wall that was and is built between Truth and Illusion, that billows in the parentheses – the (true) and (false) at the end of each item in the Perceptual Aberration and Magical Ideation scales – telling us the 'right' answer. A divide that, as also introduced in Chapter 4, is filled with fears that we might, and thus moral imperatives that we shall not, 'regress' to soft, illusory beliefs shamefully lying far from the hard truth of progress – for the colonizer-Scientist is "he who *knows* how to distinguish the *real* from the *false* . . ." (Trinh, 1989, p. 56, her emphasis). Such "setting of an absolute boundary, a clear dividing line, a geometry of exclusion that positions the self on one side, and the other – the not-self – on the other side" exemplifies a colonial logic (Barad, 2014, p. 169), that abyss carved into the stranger's face that Anzaldúa (1987) saw in the black, obsidian mirror of the Nahuas.

> The gaping mouth slit heart from mind. Between the two eyes in her head, the tongueless magical eye and the loquacious rational eye, was la rajadura, the abyss that no bridge could span. Separated, they could not visit each other and each was too far away to hear what the other

was saying. Silence rose like a river and could not be held back. It flooded and drowned everything.

(p. 66–67)

This drowning silence echoes in the experience of "'solitary consciousness,' and its mute, disenchanted world," that, as per Stengers (2011), "the bifurcation of nature turned into the only rational starting point for inquiry" (p. 353). Prodrome-the-borderland suggests that this colonial interference may not have only displaced our participation with the world, but diffracted it too – producing not the same elsewhere, so much as something else (Barad, 2007). Living in the borderland, Anzaldúa's Coatlicue whispers these missed connections in our ears. Yet, heard in a neocolonial security state awash with fear, her otherworldly correspondence becomes cryptic, shameful, overwhelming, growing as paranoia like a "crystal in a hyper-saturated solution" (Sedgwick, 2003, p. 131). Standing at the gates of psycurity, it is only allowed entry to reality when stamped by the SIPS with Psychotic Disorder: detained in our individualized psyches, blocked at the border, "That writhing serpent movement, the very movement of life, swifter than lightening, frozen" (Anzaldúa, 1987, p. 42). Within the prodromal movement our imagination encounters not just what Miranda Fricker (2008) calls an 'epistemic injustice,' but some sort of ontologic one too – repeating an obliteration central to the colonial project (Bhabha, 2004).

Yet again, the prodrome is potentially more than this. For Stengers (2012), everything requires a specific milieu in order for it to exist and, on the flipside, not everything may accept the milieu that is offered to it. Experiences that might be explained (away) as "superstition, belief, or symbolic efficacy" – such as those checked by psycurity through the prodromal movement – might be better seen as requiring a milieu that "does not answer to scientific demands" (p. 3). Anzaldúa's Coatlicue shows us that our questioning of the prodrome could move towards, "kicking a hole out of the old boundaries of the self and slipping under or over, dragging the old skin along, stumbling over it" (1987, p. 71). This strange goddess suggests that there *is* something else right here, right now; that "slightly alien guest" within paranoia's own (linguistic) ancestry (Miller, 1977).

Beside-the-mind

I see oposicion e insurrection. I see the crack growing on the rock. I see the fine frenzy building. I see the heat of anger or rebellion or hope split open that rock, releasing la Coatlicue. And someone in me takes matters into our own hands, and eventually, takes dominion

over serpents – over my body, my sexual activity, my soul, my mind, my weaknesses and strengths. Mine. Ours. Not the heterosexual white man's or the colored man's or the state's or the culture's or the religion's or the parents' – just ours, mine.
And suddenly I feel everything rushing to a center, a nucleus. All the lost pieces of myself come flying from the deserts and the mountains and the valleys, magnetized toward that center. Completa.
Something pulsates in my body, a luminous thin thing that grows thicker every day. Its presence never leaves me. I am never alone. That which abides: my vigilance, my thousand sleepless serpent eyes blinking in the night, forever open. And I am not afraid.

(Anzaldúa, 1987, p. 73)

Cradled in the arms of Coatlicue, the prodrome points to the vitality and the milieu of paranoia, changing the shape of this experience from cliff-edge to borderland, from individual to ecology. Beside-the-mind not only takes us to paranoia's space of encounter and the objects and operations that make this up; it takes us to paranoia's unruliness. Treating threshold phenomenon as capacities that shapeshift across different situations – perhaps colonizing, perhaps decolonizing, perhaps something else – it encourages an 'ethological approach.' In some ways similar to Brown and Stenner's (2009) suggestion that we watch and learn how the whale-*cum*-psyche behaves in different circumstances, an ethological approach also understands that what we follow is not indifferent to how we engage with it, that it may actively prevent us from getting a hold (Pignarre & Stengers, 2011). Beside-the-mind, then, takes the whale's agency into account, too. Indeed, it suggests that paranoia may be looking back at Psychology, "my thousand sleepless serpent eyes blinking in the night, forever open" (Anzaldúa, 1987, p. 73).

Choosing not to take the line offered by the SIPS, plunging vertically through the border between imagination and reality, is not anti-empiricism. Quite the opposite. It calls for a 'more extreme' kind, refusing to privilege mechanisms that are "otherwise used to judge or measure according to a norm, differentiating between experiences whose objects are legitimate or illusory" (Stengers, 2011, p. 234). Withholding eliminative judgment, instruments like the SIPS can be invited instead to identify the very experiences that will be, as Anzaldúa (1987) writes in her poetry, "the green shoot that cracks the rock" (p. 105). Far from the bifurcation of nature, it is perhaps *this* splitting – of Psychology's episteme – that we might seek when engaging the prodrome. An unsettling, reparative reading that suggests existing prodromal tools may not necessarily "bring in psychological individualism through the back door" (Blackman et al., 2008, p. 10). Indeed, that with certain interlocutors they may even hold a potential to 're-turn' (Barad, 2014) paranoia's etymological roots.

Roots that, pointing to an otherworldly correspondence in the coils of psycurity itself, further imply a source of fresh air within a neocolonial security state. Unlike the paranoia outlined by Sedgwick (2003), beside-the-mind entices a *mystified* view of systemic oppressions, thus perhaps also reclaiming paranoia as a potential medium of political or cultural struggle. Through Anzaldúa's (1987) Coatlicue, we are reminded that this sense of the world is telling us that something else lies nearby. Far from hunting or even just following this experience, then, we might pursue an apprenticeship with it, "creating new means of grasping a situation, leading to the production of new ways of acting, of connecting, of being efficacious . . ." (Pignarre & Stengers, 2011, p. 77). Beside-the-mind allows paranoia to be a little green snake, hissing both cause and cure, soliciting a different kind of response-ability for Psychology within suffocating conditions: no longer, *What is the matter* with *paranoia? What should we do about it?*, so much as *What is the matter of paranoia? What else could it do?* In the following chapter I put this imaginative leap to the test.

Notes

1 A longer version of this chapter was originally published in *Subjectivity*. It has been reprinted with permission from Springer Nature (see Liebert, 2017a).
2 According to Anna-Louise Keating (2009), Gloria Anzaldúa's writing on Coatlicue is rarely excerpted or examined yet "these issues were crucial to Anzaldúa herself and represent some of the most innovative, visionary dimensions of her work" (p. 5). Anzaldúa explicitly wrote how her words did not 'belong' to her; that once they came though her body and onto the page they were there for people to pick up and use, to think and leap with. At the same time with regard to Indigenous spiritualities, while "some things are worth borrowing," we "often misuse what we've borrowed by using it out of context" and thus "need to scrutinize the purpose and accountability for one's 'borrowing'" (Anzaldúa, 2002, p. 289). In this essay I risk isolating Coatlicue, disconnecting her from Mexica culture and land, forcing her into a Western context – effectively treating her, as Anzaldúa (2002) continues, in a manner akin to how colonial museums exhibit Indigenous objects. By committing to decolonizing content and politics and experimenting with an unsettling form and practice, I hope that I have been able to host Coatlicue in a respectful way, maintaining her liveliness (Hillman, 1975) and opacity (Trinh, 1989). Nonetheless, I am walking a dangerous line of 'inclusion.' This endnote is to witness and enter – without resolving/dissolving – my accountability in doing so.
3 I am reminded here of an article in the *Psychiatric Times* on November 14, 2014, about Dr John Mack, a Harvard Professor who came to accept that his patients' reports of alien abductions were accurate recounts of real events, inciting "decidedly negative reactions" from his colleagues for "going native" (n.p.).
4 From A. N. Whitehead, *Adventure of Ideas* (New York: Free Press, 1967).
5 From A. N. Whitehead, *Process and Reality* (New York: Free Press, 1979).
6 From A. N. Whitehead, *Science and the Modern World* (New York: Free Press, 1967).
7 From A. N. Whitehead, *Process and Reality* (New York: Free Press, 1979).

DRAWING 5. "Breathing." Black ink on cochineal print, el Jardín Etnobotánico de Oaxaca. Rachel Jane Liebert, 2016.

6
COMPOST

For Frantz Fanon (1952), colonization is the "worm-eaten roots" of society that need to be excavated and expelled (p. 4). Yet where there are worm-eaten roots, there are worms:

> We might imagine re-turning as a multiplicity of processes, such as the kinds earthworms revel in while helping to make compost or otherwise being busy at work and at play: turning the soil over and over – ingesting and excreting it, tunnelling through it, burrowing, all means of aerating the soil, allowing oxygen in, opening it up and breathing new life into it.
>
> *(Barad, 2014, p. 168)*

This quote from Karen Barad (2014) suggests that the worms of coloniality might be able to guide us in 're-turning' its roots, aerating what are otherwise conditions of breathlessness (Maldonado-Torres, 2016). In Chapter 4 I suggest that, within psycurity, the neocolonial security state is animated by paranoia. Re-turning paranoia's roots may thus breathe new life into this suffocating state. Following the reparative reading offered in Chapter 5, this latent liveliness is imagination, an otherworldly correspondence exiled through coloniality's 'de-supernaturalizing' of our modes of being human (Wynter, 2003). The practices of worms, then, could perhaps offer guidance for turning the matter of paranoia into imagination. Moreover, given that our de-supernaturalization is re-inscribed through Science, Sylvia Wynter (2003) suggests that one might interrupt it by joining Science with art. And so, in what follows, I put my experience of a collaboration with a visual artist into proximity with worms to theorize re-turning the roots of paranoia. More specifically, I take on a creative apprenticeship with paranoia vis-à-vis a measure of its potential – the Magical Ideation scale – to learn how one might make space for imagination within a neocolonial security state. Composting psycurity, this experiment offers Psychology fresh modes of response-ability, within contemporary conditions.

Space-making

At the center of the worldwide prodromal movement, the Structured Interview for Psychosis-Risk Syndromes (SIPS) is designed to identify the prodrome, a pre-psychotic state that includes potential paranoia (Miller et al., 2002). It is the descendant of several scales including Magical Ideation – introduced in Chapter 5 and formally defined as, "the belief, quasi-belief, or semi-serious entertainment of the possibility that events which, according to the causal concepts of this culture, cannot have a causal relation with each other, might somehow nevertheless do so" (Eckblad & Chapman, 1983, p. 215). To construct the first and most authoritative scale for Magical Ideation, Mark Eckblad and Loren Chapman (1983) drew on clinical case studies and psychoanalytic theory, drafting 42 potential items and administering them to 227 undergraduates along with tests of acquiescence and social desirability, where those items that correlated too highly were made "more specific" or "less embarrassing," respectively. A revised scale was then given to two successive samples of undergraduates – 373 people in total – before being revised again to reach their final 30 true/false items, launching a trajectory of "pre-schizophrenic" research that led Loren Chapman and Jean Chapman, a decade later, to receive the American Psychological Association award for Distinguished Scientific Applications of Psychology.

In the previous chapter I refused to take a line offered by the SIPS, to split reality and imagination. Instead, I followed the direction of Isabelle Stengers (2011) and took an 'imaginative leap' that put prodromal research into conversation with a more-than-human voice typically not allowed through the gates of psycurity – Anzaldúa's (1987) Coatlicue. This strange goddess redirected attention to not just the liveliness of paranoia's potential but also its poisoned milieu, inviting an apprenticeship with paranoia, a finding of new ways of being efficacious by "learning the antidotes against what has been poisoned, and continues to poison, the situation" (Pignarre & Stengers, 2011, p. 95). This poison is the divide between Truth and Illusion inscribed during colonization and enacted in the Magical Ideation scale's determination of people's experiences as True or False. To take on an apprenticeship with paranoia is in part to learn how one might treat this incision.

For Stengers (2012), this requires 'thinking by the milieu.' That is, to turn our gaze away from the truthiness of Magical Ideation, casting a judgment from a place of Knowing, and toward the conditions that welcome it, or not, or somewhat. Unlike Eckblad and Chapman's (1983) definition of Magical Ideation above, such an approach "would not dream of addressing others in terms of the 'beliefs' they entertain about a 'reality' to which scientists enjoy privileged access" (Stengers, 2012, p. 2). Indeed Stengers (2012) places thinking by the milieu against the "scientific conquering 'view of the world'" introduced in Chapter 4, a colonizing Science (in the singular and with a big 'S') that appears "bent on translating everything that exists into objective, rational knowledge" (p. 2), throwing a think-net over the world, disciplining it, settling it. Instead, thinking by the milieu recognizes that milieu make demands of that which they are trying to represent – demands that will not necessarily be accepted. For example, in Eckblad and Chapman's (1983) abovementioned process for developing the Magical Ideation scale, the high rates of 'acquiescence' could be indicative of the experiences resonating with people (not simply their tendency toward suggestibility); the high rates of 'social desirability' could be indicative of the experiences being shameful for people (not simply their tendency to give pleasing responses). The possibility of these interpretations forces attention to the milieu of Magical Ideation, to the ecological conditions that shut down these experiences, exposing them to ontologic injustice.

An experiment, then, can be less a test of the object of inquiry, than of the milieu itself. In turn, Stengers (2011) calls for an 'adventure of the sciences' (in the plural and with a small 's') that involves the "creation of a situation enabling what the scientists question to put their question at risk, to make the difference between relevant questions and unilaterally imposed ones" (p. 2). Within this "very particular creative art," objects of inquiry become "enrolled as a 'partner'" (p. 2), such that sciences become a craft of making spaces that animate our objects, allowing them to test our tests. Such questioning of the questioners is a key tactic in contemporary decolonizing movements, which are increasingly targeting institutions that make, claim, inflict Truth (Maldonado-Torres, 2016). Disobeying dichotomies of Knower and Known, delinking narratives of progress and civilization, Stengers' art-form is thus perhaps also an opening for sciences to do 'aestheSis' (with the unsettled 'S'; Mignolo & Vázquez, 2013) – a praxis that not only "perceives the wound of coloniality hidden under the rhetoric of modernity" but "moves towards the healing, the recognition, the dignity of those aesthetic practices that have been written out of the canon of modern aestheTics" (n.p.).

Not only perceiving the wound of Truth and Illusion but moving toward witnessing a more-than-human vitality otherwise whitewashed within the colonial episteme, *Missed Connections* became a multimedia attempt at this kind of craft. I collaborated with visual artist Holli McEntegart,[1] to undertake an apprenticeship with paranoia by turning to Magical Ideation, learning how psychologies (in the plural and with a small 'p') might welcome paranoia's choked potentials. During December 2014, a first iteration was performed in the US. Daily anonymous postings of Magical Ideation statements were placed on New York's Craigslist Missed Connections (a public website for realizing romantic and deviant fantasies), coupled with an email address for private responses, mapped to a physical location around New York City, scribed there in pencil, photographed, left to be rubbed off by elements or touch. Inspired by the US Department of Homeland Security's 'anti-terror' campaign "If you see something, say something," physical locations were randomly chosen during my daily commutes, echoing a banal everyday suspicion. During October 2015, a second iteration was performed in Aotearoa New Zealand. Daily anonymous postings of Magical Ideation statements were placed on Auckland's Craigslist Missed Connections, coupled with an email address for private responses, mapped to a physical location around the city, scribed there with pencil, photographed, left to be rubbed off by elements or touch. Inspired by the 1907 Tohunga Suppression Act (TSA; as introduced in Chapter 1), physical locations were specifically chosen to echo dis-membered dreams (see Plates 1–8).[2]

Spurred by a recurring picture in my head and a voice from Holli's gut, *Missed Connections* grew from a collision of imagination, more followed than directed. Moving between one of the older and one of the newer settler colonies of the British Empire, it soon obliged attention to the coloniality of the milieu, as well as to the constitutive role of space in the making of things. Both of which invoked Barad's (2007) onto-epistemology of 'agential realism,' which rests on a recognition that *"we are part of that nature that we seek to understand"* (p. 67, her emphasis). It follows that theorizing itself is not "a spectator sport of matching linguistic representation to preexisting things" (p. 54), so much as a material practice of experimentation. Placing it beside Psychology, *Missed Connections* changed the context, the experimental apparatus, of Magical Ideation, helping me to think by the milieu, to theorize how space-making could be a mode of response-ability for psychologies seeking decoloniality. And thus to learn about not only re-turning paranoia's roots, but Psychology's – that breathless study of *psykhe* – too.

Re-turning

In the opening quote to this chapter, Barad (2014) enlists re-turning to talk about diffraction – "not only a lively affair, but one that troubles dichotomies" (p. 168). A sort of fractal reckoning of diffraction with itself, re-turning offers a spiraling methodology made up of 'intra-actions.' Unlike relationships that are defined by *inter*actions, presuming two or more pre-existing entities coming and acting together, intra-actions *make things*, enacting "agential cuts" that do not create absolute separations so much as "cut together-apart (one move)" (p. 168). Through intra-action, elements *both* come together *and* become separate, thus approaching 'entities' as 'entanglements':

> Each bit of matter, each moment of time, each position in space is a multiplicity, a superposition/entanglement of (seemingly) disparate parts. Not a blending of separate parts or a blurring of boundaries, but in the thick web of its specificities, what is at issue is its unique material historialities and how they come to matter.
> *(Barad, 2014, p. 176)*

With diffraction, *all* phenomena (including supposedly disturbed perceptions) are entangled material agencies, a multiplicity of everything that is intra-acting to create them. Not creating unity, erasing difference – enacting difference. And thus attuning to how differences come to matter.

In turn, entanglements affect response-ability. For one, queering boundaries, they direct attention to otherness *within* – as happened in Chapter 5, where paranoia was invited as a kind of 'threshold phenomena' (Blackman, 2014), a 'borderland' (Anzaldúa, 1987) vibrating with agential realism, with diffraction. As mentioned above, this reading welcomed imagination – otherworldly correspondence – as part of paranoia's potential. In doing so it pointed to the possibility of a 'space of disjunct' within the coils of psycurity itself – that is, the potential to make something hopeful out of the fearful matter of paranoia (McManus, 2011). For Susan McManus (2011), one strategy for such 'affective restructuring' might be turning technologies that are central to the production of fear against themselves; in this case, turning the tools that are used in psycurity back on psycurity, such that "fear is put to work in helpful ways" (n.p.). In what follows, then, with the Magical Ideation scale, I attempt to articulate how one might re-turn paranoia's borderland soil, unearthing pockets of imagination. I attend to my experience of *Missed Connections* to turn paranoia's potential over and over again, reflexively musing on what the experiment's multiplicity of processes – its own ingesting/excreting, tunneling, and burrowing – taught me about breathing new life into paranoia, and thus offered for psychological praxis within a neocolonial security state.

Ingesting/excreting: mystery

Ingest: *Transitive verb*: to take in for or as if for digestion

Excrete: *Transitive verb*: to separate and eliminate or discharge (waste) from the blood, tissues, or organs or from the active protoplasm.

The craft of worms is in their digestion. With a mouth but no teeth, they take decaying matter in one end of their tubular bodies, break it down with moisture, microorganisms, and muscle, absorb what they need and release what is insoluble out the other end. It is these recycled 'castings' that, containing nitrogen and other nutrients, nourish the soil, preparing the ground for new plant growth. If their tail is severed they grow another, when they die they digest each other. Hermaphrodites that can breed alone, there are over one million worms for every acre of land, said to have collectively digested every bit of fertile soil on earth. Underground, they are unseen to our eyes and un-needing of their own, although sensitive to light and touch. Eating waste and wasting food, death before life and life after death, both female and male, creating without vision, worms' ingesting/excreting intra-acts the im/possible to fertilize conditions for something else.

Presenting an item on the Magical Ideation scale in a list (see Plate 1), as a post (see Plate 1), on the world (see Plates 2–8), then switching to the next, *Missed Connections* was a montage, a series of fragments placed alongside one another. Escaping linear narrative or pre-given concepts or categories, it provoked curiosity, questions, meaning-making. It demanded participation. Yet the wide range of responses it solicited through Craigslist – flirting, anger, confusion, fear, censorship, silence – were given no answer. *Missed Connections* generated more questions. It released something lively. At the same time, having entered the world with no explanation, no mention, indeed with no vision, *Missed Connections* required surrendering to not knowing where something was going. If anywhere – the posts disappeared from Craigslist after 45 days, the pencil disappeared from the world after rain, wind, snow, sea, touch. Too slippery to grip, the items of Magical Ideation were unknowable, obliging a multisensory groping in the dark, feeling (not seeing) the way. *Missed Connections* became about experimentation. Putting stuff out in public and seeing what happened. Including nothing. Riding my bicycle, re-cycling day after day, the experimentation of *Missed Connections* necessitated endurance, struggle. Continuing rain or shine or snow, it demanded the help of others. Passing things through, passing things along, bodies along, in order to pass the possibilities of Magical Ideation along. A kind of communal metabolism. Ingesting the Magical Ideation scale with no teeth, breaking it down into smaller pieces, and excreting something insoluble, ready for collective participation, *Missed Connections* fertilized conditions for something else.

Evoking a continual escaping, questioning, surrendering, experimenting, collectivizing, my experience with *Missed Connections* pointed me toward a practice of *mystery* for fertilizing spaces within psycurity. Contrary to being the antithesis of 'hard science,' mystery is stirring in contemporary approaches in neuroscience (e.g., Roy, 2016), botany (e.g., Myers, 2015) and physics (where mystery is "alive and well"; Barad, 2014), where – at least below the surface – it is breathing life into one's objects of inquiry, witnessing their vitality. Moreover, for Gabriel Marcel (1995), mystery brings a capacity to provoke an infinite line of questioning, thus shifting one's role away from figuring out The Answer – denying the dynamism of the world – to being an interlocutor. While not using the language of 'mystery,' Tobie Nathan (1999) similarly tasks psychologies to "always create fruitful material, open to elaboration, to new productions, to life" (n.p.) and has found it necessary to enlist a 'contradictor' to do so – a partner or two or more that can help us question what we think and do, preventing us from biting down on it with the 'big teeth' of 'big concepts' (Pignarre & Stengers, 2011). In this context, 'critique' is not an attack against which we defend theories and methods so much as a form of collaboration to protect the liveliness of both practice and the world.

In turn, a problem is that which works to 'gather together,' not be (re)solved, and practice becomes a sort of 'relay,' "an itinerant definition of success, reinventing itself whenever a situation changes, assembling communities of new types of objectors (not sharing the same obligations)" (Pignarre & Stengers, 2011, p. 125). Rather than solutions, mystery invites responses in the form of trial and error, animating our response-ability with a commitment to collective experimentation. It thus perhaps offers psychologies a means to break the cycle of 'epistemological violence' otherwise looming from the declarative authority of Science in our praxis (Teo, 2010). Indeed, compromising Knowing, mystery invites the presence of what Stengers (2012) calls 'magic.' While typically used to derogate efficacy, my experience with mystery suggested that this presence – etymologically deriving from *magh*, 'to be able' – offers to capacitate psychologies. To admit magic is to surrender to not Knowing, to things not being Knowable; an admission necessary for imagination. Anzaldúa (1987), for example, considers her practice of writing – whether theory, story, or poetry – as an encounter with something more-than-human that first requires her to "let the walls fall down" (p. 97). These walls are those that demarcate the borders between worlds; Anzaldúa's surrendering guides her through/to otherworldly correspondence. Mystery offers to breathe new life into a space.

Intra-acting what is im/possible, mystery in turn enacts an indifference to colonial theorizing, to "piercing . . . through the sediments of psychological and epistemological 'depths'" (Trinh, 1989, p. 48). Here, Trinh Minh-ha (1989) is instead advocating for respecting the "realm of opaqueness" that comes with a "foreign thing"; an ongoing opacity that in turn generates conditions for an ongoing questioning – declared by Fanon (1952) as necessary for anticolonial revolution. Mystery thus enables a kind of decolonizing deference that perhaps also helps with 'smelling the smoke,' with feeling a discomfort from that present colonial past of hunting and burning, diagnosing and treating, as though we Know (Stengers, 2012). At the same time, approaching everyone as captured by this lineage, mystery allows for us to unashamedly need each other – setting the "bar of reason" as "not a privileged epistemic subject but an intersubjective community: the whole world" (Maldonado-Torres, 2006, p. 128). In this way, mystery also aligns with the 'border thinking' introduced in Chapter 1, with choosing interlocutors who could open us to readings that lie beside a colonial episteme (Mignolo, 2012). Digesting the world in ways that are humble, participatory, and communal, mystery offers to metabolize the soil of paranoia, re-turning its roots within a neocolonial security state. In doing so, mystery could fertilize a space for otherworldly correspondence, for imagination, breathing new life into psycurity, into Psychology.

Tunneling: ritual

> Tunneling: *Intransitive verb*: To make or use a tunnel
>
> Tunnel: *Noun*. A horizontal passageway through or under an obstruction

The craft of worms is in their tunnels. Simple and segmented, their bodies move in a rhythmic pulse, shifting their front half forward, anchoring it with small hairs – 'setae' – then pulling their back half to meet it. As they move in this way through the soil, they leave body-shaped tubes in their wake. At the same time, a mucus mixed with undigested soil is secreted out their ends, lining the tubes. Through this repetitive motion of wriggling and reinforcement, a network of enduring tunnels is built that provides drainage and aeration for the soil. And, when they die, they are digested by other worms – secreted as the reinforcing mucus, becoming the tunnel they were making, continually lubricating the flow of water and air, connecting past and future. Their bodies both molding and being tunnel, worms' tunneling intra-acts it/self to structure the conditions for something else.

With statements anonymously posted online and scribed onto physical surfaces, in *Missed Connections* Magical Ideation came from the world (see Plates 2–8). The 'I' becoming *both* its readers *and* something else – the more-than-human, worming its way into perception. Yet this otherworldly vitality was dependent on a movement between registers. Literally tethering the metaphysical and the physical, the virtual and the real, the human and the non-human, *Missed Connections* demanded a daily routine. A mundane rhythm of posting, cycling, scribing, photographing. Of posting, cycling, scribing, photographing. And repeat. The liveliness of Magical Ideation required constant tending, a pedaling, spiraling labor of maintenance conducted by my body – sometimes with joy, sometimes with anxiety, sometimes with nothing, but always something. Touching base on the regular. Tunneling across worlds with mechanical movements, enacting a subterranean connectedness, *Missed Connections* directed an embodied approach for nourishing the more-than-human, structuring conditions for something else.

Simple, repeated, embodied, tending, my experience with *Missed Connections* pointed me toward a practice of *ritual* for structuring spaces within psycurity, witnessing and enacting a worldly involvement. For Stengers (2012), recovering this involvement means recovering a capacity to treat experiences as not 'ours' so much as a beholding of something more-than-human, as 'animating' us. Yet, locating subjectivity only in humans, Psychology creates a 'unified front' against these experiences, thus first requiring a decentering of the human subject (Hillman, 1975). Nathan (1999), for example, approaches madness as "manufactured by things" – whether ideas, objects, operations, encounters – thereby redirecting his practice toward learning "to handle" these things, to "look after them, feed them, all the while receiving sustenance from them" (n.p.). Likewise for Anzaldúa (1987), witnessing a more-than-human vitality obliges treating it as having "the same needs as a person, it needs to be 'fed'" (p. 89). For her, such feeding happens through ritual – simple, repeated, embodied actions that give physical visible form to metaphysical invisible forces. Indeed without ritual, something risks being, "a dead 'thing' separated from nature and, therefore, its power" (p. 90).

Ritual thus does not simply acknowledge the more-than-human, it enlivens it – opening possibilities for otherworldly correspondence, for imagination. For Hillman (1975), this openness is only possible if we also learn not how to make imagination our object so much as how to become *its* object, "giving over to the images and cultivating them for their sake" (p. 40). Not just watching and listening, but caretaking as they come and go. Ritual offers psychologies a way of taking care – an everyday labor that not only nourishes the more-than-human and our relationality, but also invites an experience of an agency that pulls 'us' into being – that is, an experience of magic (Stengers, 2012), of "a force that obliges one to think/feel/act" (Pignarre & Stengers, 2011, p. 135). Crucially, such a practice can also involve words. At once able to capture, tame and appropriate "the intangible as human" (Trinh, 1989, p. 53), words also make things matter (Barad, 2007) – a power well-known by discursive psychologists, Indigenous peoples, and witches, and the opposite of the Western proverb, 'Sticks and stones may break my bones, but words will never hurt me' (Elder, 2015). My experience with ritual suggested treating words – including those used in the Magical Ideation scale – as incantations. In turn, psychologies' diagnostics – whether of problems or people – can be seen as not determining *what is* so much as bringing into being a connection with *what else*. Ritual offers to breathe new life into a space.

Witnessing and enacting our worldly involvement, intra-acting it/self, ritual diffracts humanity across colonial borders, gently restoring an 'ontological obliteration' central to the colonial project (Bhabha, 2004). Moreover its caretaking works as a kind of giving that, unlike the 'imperial gift,' animates the receiver (Maldonado-Torres, 2006); its embodiment works as a connective tissue that elevates the flesh, destabilizing the Cartesian hierarchy of capitalism, colonialism, white supremacy; and its repetitiveness leaves a trace that joins time and space. All of which prevent a stuck-ness in one place or another, disturbing a linearity that is otherwise inhospitable to decolonizing possibilities (Rowe & Tuck, 2016). As Barad (2014), also drawing on Anzaldúa, writes, "tunneling through boundaries" is "not a bloodless but a necessary revolutionary political action" (p. 175), for it is "not only that we live in many worlds at the same time, but also that these worlds are, in fact, all in the same place – the place each one of us is here and now" (p. 176). Clearing the airways between human and more-than-human, colonial and more-than-colonial, ritual offers to unblock the soil of paranoia, re-turning its roots within a neocolonial security state. In doing so, ritual could structure a space for otherworldly correspondence, for imagination, breathing new life into psycurity, into Psychology.

Burrowing: pausing

> Burrow: *noun*: a hole or excavation in the ground made by an animal (such as a rabbit) for shelter and habitation.
>
> Burrowing: *intransitive verb*: to conceal oneself in or as if in a burrow.
>
> *The craft of worms is in their burrows. Breathing through their moist skin, they struggle when things are too frozen, too hot, too bright – they become paralyzed if*

exposed to light for more than an hour. To evade these dry conditions, they dig down into the soil – up to six feet deep – and excavate a chamber with their bodies, lining it with a mucous to keep them moist, to help them breathe. To survive over prolonged periods, they use these burrows to curl into a tight ball, anchor themselves with their setae, and enter a reduced metabolic state – 'aestivation' – waiting until the context becomes less suffocating. On the flip side, they will shift to overground when conditions are especially favorable – after rain or during high humidity – creating a mass movement that swiftly reaches new ground. Burrowing is also the means by which worms incubate their eggs, leaving them alone to survive even extreme weather until the babies sense it is safe to hatch and grow. Sheltering breath outside yet inside suffocating conditions, making a microcosm in order to make a macrocosm, worms' burrowing intra-acts un/favorable to sustain conditions for something else.

By slipping Magical Ideation into not just Craigslist, but the beach, the construction site, the subway, the tourist spot, the strip-joint, the canon, the suburban street – *Missed Connections* excavated a space for the unexpected within the expected (see Plates 1–8). Written in places of both reality and fantasy, both fear and desire, these statements could shelter outside yet inside a milieu that otherwise designated them as Normal or Psychotic, retaining their liveliness. Yet at the same time, the (true) or (false) billowing at the end of each statement suggested the casting of this dichotomizing, immobilizing light nearby. Sensing the dangers of judgment, *Missed Connections* invited digging down and staying in the darkness, waiting. Stretched over months, it adopted a regular but slow pace, nestling into the cracks of time and space yet paying attention, giving Magical Ideation a chance amidst suffocating conditions. Sustaining the conditions for something else.

Sheltering, sensing, waiting, slowing, attending my experience with *Missed Connections* pointed me toward a practice of *pausing* for sustaining spaces within psycurity. La Prieta – a character from Anzaldúa's short stories – suggests in an interview with Anzaldúa (n.d.) that she keeps falling through cracks because "it's dangerous to get too rigid and fixated on a certain kind of reality – that this reality is not all it appears to be. There are cracks in the picture," that "other worlds exist and they sometimes bleed into this one through the cracks" (p. 275). These cracks echo in what Stengers (2011) calls 'interstices' – moments of more-than-human intrusion that suspend habits and solicit hesitation, a "precarious sense of the possible" (Pignarre & Stengers, 2011, p. 112). The power of these cracks is not in their revelation that there are cracks in the picture so much as in their revelation that the picture can crack. A practice of pausing, then, provides a refuge for this trembling sense, this gasp of air; interstices are not something that we make so much as shelter. Specifically, Stengers continues, they require a milieu that is protected from binaries. This kind of shelter is threatened within

Psychology by everyday practices such as interpretation, which translates experiences into "ready-made theoretical tokens" (Nathan, 1999, n.p.). The challenge for psychologies is thus to not respond with a pre-conceived, over-arching judgment, but to treat each experience as it comes, allowing its own immanent unfolding. That is, to give a chance – "the suspension of the probable, the holding out of a chance for the possible" (Pignarre & Stengers, 2011, p. 66). Pausing is perhaps a means to create this kind of breathing space, receptive to – and for – more-than-human intrusions, otherworldly correspondence.

For Anzaldúa (1986) another world "crops up when we least expect it" (p. 106), "speaks to us in the moments when we are least aware" (p. 108). Again guided by Anzaldúa, Barad (2014) further writes that there "is no absolute outside; the outside is always already inside. In/determinacy is an always already opening up-to-come. In/determinacy is the surprise, the interruption, by the stranger (within) re-turning unannounced" (p. 178). Pausing may thus enable psychologies to make a space for these scholars' un/expected outside inside by taking on a kind of paradoxical vigilance – an 'empiricism on alert' that aims to be caught off-guard, that is ready to be surprised (Stengers, 2011). In turn, pausing too invites an "art of immanent attention" to "what is good and what is toxic", to consequences rather than causes. My experience with pausing allowed for this kind of magic (Stengers, 2012, p. 8). Making a hole for imagination – Anzaldúa's (2002) 'la hoya' – it is a place where ideas can be "stirred and cooked to a new integration" (p. 292), creating microcosms for practicing and incubating another world. Pausing offers to breathe new life into a space.

Intra-acting the un/favorable, pausing makes a space not poisoned by a colonial lineage of this or that, casting a judgment as though we Know, but opening to a both/and. Far from idleness or apathy, it exemplifies the rigorous labor required of decolonizing work, where Maldonado-Torres (2016) describes "there is no place for laziness" (p. 11) – "Nothing can be automatically embraced as constructive and empowering; not everything can be rejected as a pure instrument of coloniality" (p. 11). Pausing appreciates that there is neocolonial in the decolonial and decolonial in the neocolonial. Encouraging a sharpened sensibility to shifty conditions, this 'aesthetics of interruption' is particularly necessary within a colonial episteme built on ignorance (Watkins & Shulman, 2008). Indeed, it is perhaps an ally of what Anzaldúa (2001) describes as 'border art' – that which pokes holes in imposed worlds, allowing an "exten[sion] beyond the confines of our skin, situation, and condition" (p. 248). Making breathing space within suffocating conditions, incubating liveliness, creating microcosms, pausing offers to build shelters in the soil of paranoia, re-turning its roots within a neocolonial security state. In doing so, pausing could sustain a space for otherworldly correspondence, for imagination, breathing new life into psycurity, into Psychology.

Magical ideation

Fertilizing, structuring, and sustaining the space, putting my experience of *Missed Connections* into proximity with worms suggested that practices of mystery, ritual, and pausing may work together to turn the roots of paranoia over and over again, breathing new life into it. Allowing fresh air to come through ritual, be sheltered within pausing, and be metabolized through mystery, these three practices offer to make a space for otherworldly correspondence, for imagination, within suffocating conditions. Working from an agential realism that treats experiences as entanglements, the experiment diffracted the im/possible, it/self, and the un/favorable, directing attention to differences here-now and how these come to matter. In particular, given a context of psycurity, this composting opened a space for the decolonial in the neocolonial.[3] Mystery, ritual, and pausing thus offer a tactic for composting not only psycurity but Psychology too – reviving response-abilities for psychologies within a neocolonial security state.

Further, by respectively obliging a compromise on what we Know, one to think/feel/act, and an art of immanent attention, mystery, ritual, and pausing suggest magic might be a driving force behind such composting. For Stengers (2012), magic offers an antidote to our poisoned milieu for even the word itself "cannot be uttered . . . with impunity" (p. 134) – describing a craft as such warns of our descent from colonizers who violently desired, claimed to Know. Moreover, typically used as metaphor, 'magic' resists capture, protecting practices from becoming yet another think-net. Mystery, ritual, and pausing can thus be thought of as a tactic for invoking magic-driven creation, a kind of *magical ideation* that makes a space for otherworldly correspondence. My experience of *Missed Connections* ultimately invited me to respond to psycurity, to the present political moment, by adopting an explicitly magical craft – a tactic that itself is lively enough to slip through the grip of Psychology, allowing psychologies to do a praxis that is *of* the imagination, not *on* it. Not disciplining, settling it; *making space for it*. Witnessing and welcoming a magic in the air that invites an experimentation here-now, such a tactic of magical ideation offers to not just compost but enchant the present (Pignarre & Stengers, 2011) – animating a response-ability both creative and militant in times of intensifying white supremacy, of breathlessness.

It is now two years since I first put my experience of *Missed Connections* into proximity with worms and learned about mystery, ritual, and pausing.

Over this time, I have been testing out this tactic in my own psychological praxis of healing, pedagogy, and protest within a neocolonial security state. In these spaces, which I do not separate from one another, I have found a commitment to magical ideation increasingly useful. Mystery has helped me to respond to a demand for solutions used to refuse an engagement with problems, a lingering individualism, and assumptions that one does or should Know; ritual has helped me to respond to a tendency to prioritize cognition, an ignoring of the flesh and the more-than-human, a splintering of relationships, and a forgetting of what drives us from the past and from the future; pausing has helped me to respond to pressures for productivity, and to increasing trends toward being judgmental and exclusive that are otherwise undermining the safety of these supposed 'safe spaces.' In turn, magical ideation has enabled me to make spaces that are both uncomfortable and generative, open to imagination, to that more-than-human, more-than-colonial correspondence that whispers another world is not only possible, but here-now. In conditions of intensifying white supremacy, with people feeling increasingly despondent or terrified, these modes of being human – both creative and militant – have felt at times like a breath of fresh air.

Notes

1 Holli's praxis is in part guided by family lore – passed down by stories but unable to be 'proven' – that her great-grandmother was stolen as a child from her Indigenous family and raised as white by settlers. Nowadays referred to as 'The Stolen Generation,' this was an official, systematic program of kidnapping carried out by the Australian government under the British empire to erase indigeneity and complete the process of colonization.
2 *Missed Connections* was subsequently installed in a gallery in Tamaki Makaurau Auckland and published in a book on more-than-human participation (see Brigstocke & Noorani, 2017). For more details see www.magicalideations.com.
3 Worms too: As I was looking into the practices of worms, I found a recurring claim, as exemplified in this extract from a *Journey North* website: "Experts believe most native species were wiped out wherever glaciers covered the land. Most earthworms we see today were imported mainly from Europe by early settlers. The worms or worm cocoons traveled in the rootstocks of plants brought by the settlers from their homelands. Europeans added soil, with its earthworms or worm cocoons, to ships for ballast. Once anchored in North American harbors, ships released their ballast – and living worms, who found new homes." Depicted as intrepid pioneers, hard workers who tilled a soil already empty of inhabitants, it seems even worms come with a colonizing narrative.

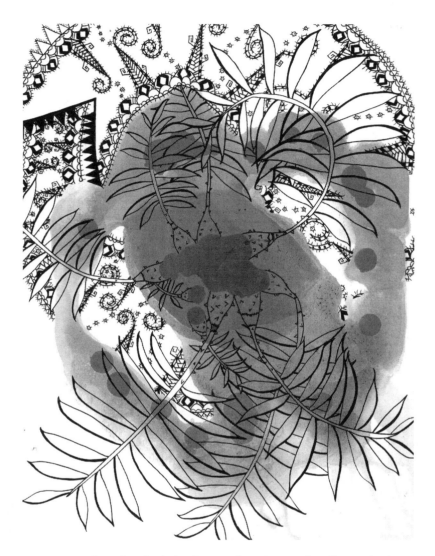

DRAWING 6. "Spiraling." Black ink on cochineal print, el Jardín Etnobotánico de Oaxaca. Rachel Jane Liebert, 2016.

7
SERPENT

In the preceding pages, I have suggested that the prodromal movement is a machine emblematic of a control society, a serpent – entering it to offer an image of paranoia as a dis-ease of white supremacy, a rationalizing, controlling, othering desire-to-know entangled with a fear-of-regressing. Hiding, predicting, branding, and growing, paranoia seeps into the cracks of white supremacy, blocking difference, an-other world. *Psycurity* is the name that I gave to the force that animates this image, an abstract machine that directs paranoia in ways that stabilize a neocolonial security state. Psycurity is paranoid stuff.

And yet this is not psycurity's only potential. In the arms of Coatlicue, a Mesoamerican goddess of the serpent, I go on to suggest that paranoia – and thus psycurity – may contain a *de*colonizing potential: imagination. What I come to understand as an *otherworldly correspondence*. That is, an openness to and dialogue with other possible worlds – 'other' as in more-than-human and more-than-colonized. A capacity to be beside-the-mind, exceeding the Psychological episteme, the colonial episteme. And thus, perhaps, something that can teach us about doing decolonizing work.

To experiment with this idea, I undertook an apprenticeship with paranoia by creatively engaging a measure of its potential, Magical Ideation. I learned how practices of mystery, ritual, and pausing may make a space for otherworldly correspondence, breathing new life into paranoia and psycurity. And I suggest that magic is the composting, enchanting force behind this space-making. A magic-driven creation, this tactic itself is a form of *magical ideation*, welcoming imagination into the paranoid coils of a neocolonial security state, aerating suffocating conditions. In what follows I consider how this all unfurled, and with what implications for psychologies.

Otherworldly correspondence

Gloria Anzaldúa (1987) writes of words as "blades of grass pushing past the obstacles, sprouting on the page; the spirit of the words moving in the body is as concrete in the flesh and as palpable" (p. 93). This project was seeded with my being drawn to a single scale, shimmering: Magical Ideation. I stumbled across it in 2012 and was immensely curious. Answering 'maybe' to first 29 and eventually 30 of its 30 'true/false' statements, there was something captivating about this self-proclaimed measure of pre-psychosis. I started, literally, to carry it around with me, reading it on commutes, talking about it with people. Over the following six years this scale became both a small piece of this project *and* the entire skin of it. In my attempts to *know* Magical Ideation, I have come to *feel* it, to *do* it. Witnessing and welcoming an entangled relationship, a partnership, with my object of inquiry as it has morphed between paranoia, imagination, magic, and, in this chapter, war. I critique paranoia with paranoia, listen to imagination with imagination, learn magical ideation with magical ideation, and, below, advocate to fight war with war. All of which is a response to the prodromal movement, a control society, a serpent. My method, like Coatlicue, has been a serpent eating its own tail, at once creation and destruction. Devouring itself.[1]

This spiraling process was not planned; it was informed, unfolding, and teaching me things about not just theorizing but doing otherworldly correspondence, breaching borders that might otherwise contain what is or should be a legitimate Psychological method. Looking back on its undulations, it has involved engaging the coloniality and whiteness usually ignored within colonial and white worlds, and engaging decolonizing theorists usually ignored by the Psychological canon; being transdisciplinary, including welcoming art as a collaborator; making the 'individual' subject of Psychology porous to the world, including welcoming embodied and inspirited knowledges; taking guidance from more-than-humans, including welcoming Coatlicue, worms, and paranoia as teachers; and entering at the point of the prodrome itself, the borderland between Normal and Psychotic. Moreover, 'psycurity,' 'otherworldly correspondence,' and 'magical ideation,' do not simply replace one think-net with another; as an abstract machine, more-than-human, and magic respectively, they are lively concepts, slipping through attempts to grip them, obliging a responsiveness that is nimble, collective, and accountable.

For Frantz Fanon (1952), to do decoloniality we need to "penetrate to a world where categories of sense and non-sense are not yet invoked" (p. 3). Categories that were cast by colonization. Creating Knowers and Known, Truth and Illusion, the smoke in our nostrils (Stengers, 2012). Generated through a kind of "spatial confrontation" between concepts – non-European and European, non-human and human, reparative and paranoid, imagination and real, magic and Science, decolonial and neocolonial – I hope that this book has pushed at the limits of territorial thinking (Mignolo, 2012), offering meanings that shimmer in-between, that "poetic knowledge" echoing in "the great silence of scientific knowledge" produced by colonization (Césaire, 1944, as translated in Kelley, 2000, p. 17). I have methodically attempted to poke at this silence with my fingertips, to make some thing stir. Not only by typing, through which ideas often come to look at me from the page, but through a more poetic style of writing[2] and – perhaps most explicitly – through drawing.

In-between the chapters of this book, out of the cracks, are ink drawings that I created during a two-month residency at el Jardín Etnobotánico in Oaxaca, Mexico. Covering two hectares in the center of Oaxaca City, el Jardín is a decolonizing project, reclaiming land occupied by missionaries then soldiers then the state, resisting commercialization of the area and corporatization of seeds, mobilizing Indigenous and sustainable praxes, and respecting plant life – both its extraordinary diversity and its entanglement with humans (de Ávila, 2006). Moreover, the design of el Jardín was a collaboration between local ethnobotanist, Alejandro de Ávila, and local surrealist artist, Francisco Toledo, thus further resonating with decoloniality given the surrealist practices of early twentieth century anti-colonial scholars (including Aimé and Suzanne Césaire; Kelley, 1999).[3] For example, in the courtyard of el Jardin, de Ávila and Toledo placed a fountain of bright red water colored by cochineal – a local bug that, when dried and ground, produces a red powder long used to make pigments in Mexico. A soft-bodied parasite, the females implant themselves on the pads of nopal cactuses for several months and drink the sap, producing a carminic acid inside their bodies that has a scarlet color. Representing blood, el Jardín's cochineal fountain was designed to speak of violence and vibrancy, the bloodshed and new blood of the land.

With a rough draft of a manuscript in hand but wanting to deepen its decoloniality, in 2016 I approached el Jardín and asked if I might spend two months writing and drawing with the plants. Having thus far worked on this book with US lands, I wanted to also spend some time with Mexican ones. This was in large part because of the influence of the work of Gloria Anzaldúa who, a Chicana philosopher and poet raised on and as the border between these two countries, was simultaneously neither and both. As an animating, borderland force behind her theorizing, it felt right to explicitly reflect this (dis)location in my process also. At the same time, I wanted to experiment with ways in which I might fold more-than-humans into my praxis. In particular, I wanted to commune with the land, to engage in dialogue about how my project connected to it, or not, or somewhat. A day after arriving, I was introduced to a local artist who recommended that I use cochineal to do so. Curious about the shifty legacy of these bugs in both reproducing and resisting colonization,[4] I spent the next two weeks searching for them, eventually being directed to an old queer Indigenous man selling rugs to tourists opposite the Catholic church in the center of the city. Curious about my request, he sat me down, handed me a small jar of dried cochineal from underneath the table, and told me how to grind them, to make different colors by adding water, lime, and baking soda, and – above all – to "go home and experiment."

Eventually,[5] I made seven cochineal presses through decalcomania. Inspired in part by the Rorschach test used in Psychology, decalcomania is a technique used by surrealists to welcome 'chance,' the cosmos into their praxis. I used trial and error to make the bugs into not only different colors but different viscosities, as I came to grind them using an unprocessed concrete pestle and half a processed coconut shell, add water, sometimes squeeze in lime, sometimes sprinkle in baking soda, pour the fresh liquid into shreds of cotton rags, squeeze it onto gloss paper, and press it with a large piece of plastic. At the same time, through people who worked at el Jardín, I was starting to hear stories about the plants, many of which had explicit links to de/colonization, and began to spiral through a daily cycle of gathering–drawing–writing. Over two months, I came to spend nearly 50 hours walking around el Jardín, doodling in a small sketchbook as a means *not* to capture or represent the plants, but to force an intimate, slow engagement with them. I would spend one or two hours each afternoon in this way, gathering textures and shapes from the plants whose stories spoke most powerfully to a concept or experience I was writing with at that time. Come sunset, I would use these gatherings to draw with black ink on a cochineal shape – one for each chapter.[6]

Each drawing took ten to 12 hours and had one question written on the back: *How does this chapter relate to the land?* As answers (often in the form of questions) came to me, I would note them down in my sketchbook, folding them back into my writing the next morning before returning to the plants to gather. And as I completed each drawing, I would have it next to me as I finalized each chapter. Turning to it for guidance. It was through this shimmering technique that sensing, smoking, seeping, bleeding, breathing, spiraling, and shapeshifting, among other processes, first came to mind. Moreover, making a space for otherworldly correspondence with the cosmos and the plants by helping to keep my project questioning of itself, tethered to the land, and attentive to more-than-humans, the drawings enabled me to put into practice mystery, ritual, and pausing. To explicitly do a kind of magical ideation. However above all, these attempts taught me about the need to go out of Psychology's comfort zone, indeed to see what feels comfortable as part of the problem (Ahmed, 2007).

War on imagination

Spiraling back to the 1907 New Zealand Tohunga Suppression Act (TSA) introduced in Chapter 1 and implicated in my ancestry, this legislation was in large part a response to Rua Kenana, a particularly powerful tohunga from Tuhōe – an iwi known for its ongoing anticolonial activism, typically referred to by past and present New Zealand government and media as 'terrorism.' Kenana was prophesizing the return of Māori land and sovereignty: Edward VII was to arrive with a gift of four million pounds (Voyce, 1989). Yet, within the settler worldview, this was patently impossible; what was threatening to colonial rule was not *what* emancipated future Kenana was foretelling, so much as *that* he was foretelling one. It was the *sense* of potential emancipation, *imagining* emancipation, to which the TSA was targeted.

A 'war on terror' appears to require a war on imagination, on that otherworldly correspondence that whispers an-other world is possible. In a preface to the twenty-first century reprint of Aimé Césaire's (1955) seminal anticolonial text, Robin Kelley (2000) writes how contemporary coloniality involves,

> The same old political parties, the same armies, the same methods of labor exploitation, the same education, the same tactics of incarceration, exiling, snuffing out artists and intellectuals who dare to imagine a radically different way of living, who dare to invent the marvellous before our very eyes.
>
> *(pp. 27–28)*

Snuffing out those who dare to imagine, to invent the marvelous, is a tactic for the neocolonial security state. With "marvellous" Kelley is invoking not Aimé but his wife, Suzanne Césaire (1941, 1943), an anti-colonial theorist and poet calling for a "permanent readiness for the Marvellous" as a strategy for revolution (as translated in Kelley, 1999, n.p.). Urging people to embrace "the domain of the strange, the marvellous and the fantastic," Césaire is particularly focused on the radical possibilities of this "freed image" within a system of colonial domination, arguing that it "nourishes an impatient strength within us, endlessly reinforcing the massive army of refusals" (n.p).

For Césaire, this nourishment comes from a "rediscovering" of "the magic power of the mahoulis, drawn directly from living sources"; one that enables a transcendence of the "sordid antinomies of the present: whites/Blacks, Europeans/Africans, civilized/savages" (n.p.). Nelson Maldonado-Torres (2016) writes of coloniality as a paradigm of war that inflicts an ontological separation on humanity, leading to 'metaphysical catastrophe' – a "transmutation of the human, from an intersubjectively constituted node of love and understanding, to an agent of perpetual or endless war" (p. 22). For him, this separation is between humans, violently splitting the world into zones of being human and zones of being sub-human. However, that this split emerged from our de-supernaturalization (Wynter, 2003) suggests that it is not just between human and human, but also between human and more-than-human, severing a force that, as per Césaire above, might otherwise help to outdo this ongoing violent process of dividing humans. Indeed, according to Isabelle Stengers (2011), interstices – those more-than-human intrusions, introduced in Chapter 6, questioning what is – become imperceptible when society mobilizes for war. Ignoring cracks in the colonial episteme, such war creates a universal, a standard, a sameness, a world as it is and must be. It is a war against an-other possible world, that which peers through the cracks, open to correspondence, here-now. And this is the work of psycurity – directing paranoia to hide, predict, brand, grow, thus seeping into the cracks, erasing difference, erasing possibility, stabilizing white supremacy. Psycurity is a war on imagination.

This takes an added twist given that paranoia has been named as a driver and effect of anti-capitalist, anti-colonial critique and action (Pignarre & Stengers, 2011; Sedgwick, 2003). The presence of paranoia suggests we may not be making space for imagination in our academic and activist praxis. If so, perhaps we are risking contribution to psycurity, to the war on imagination. Decoloniality necessitates a war against this war. In *Black Skin, White Masks*, Fanon (1952) describes the uprooting of his own decolonizing praxis, unleashing his own, surprising, revolutionary capacity:

> I had rationalized the world and the world had rejected me on the basis of color prejudice. Since no agreement was possible on the level of reason, I threw myself back toward unreason. It was up to the white man to be more irrational than I. Out of the necessities of my struggle I had chosen the method of regression, but the fact remained that it was an unfamiliar weapon; here I am at home; I am made of the irrational; I wade in the irrational. Up to the neck in the irrational. And now how my voice vibrates!
>
> *(p. 93)*

> Blood! Blood! . . . Birth! Ecstasy of becoming! Three quarters engulfed in the confusions of the day, I feel myself redden with blood. The arteries of all the world, convulsed, torn away, uprooted, have turned toward me and fed me.
>
> *(p. 95)*
>
> Black Magic, primitive mentality, animism, animal eroticism, it all floods over me. All of it is typical of people who have not kept pace with the evolution of the human race. Or, if one prefers, this is humanity at its lowest. Having reached this point, I was long reluctant to commit myself. Aggression was in the stars. I had to choose. What do I mean? I had no choice . . .
>
> *(p. 96)*

No longer up to him to be more rational than the white man, Fanon finds himself shifting the shape of the struggle. Forced to choose the method of regression, to being irrational, out of control, other. This unfamiliar weapon was prompted by Fanon's encounter with a passage by Leopold Senghor about the "rhythm" in and of Negro art. Driven by a repetition of opposites over and over again, this tyrannical symmetry creates a liveliness and difference, a "spirit" that "affects what is least intellectual in us" (p. 93). And, operating as inhalation is to exhalation, in its primordial capacity this rhythm, this animating force, is *breath*. Fanon's revolutionary capacity stirs Psychology's *psykhe*. In a neocolonial security state of rising breathlessness, psychologies – like Fanon – have no choice but to also regress, both bleeding and feeding from their roots. Going backwards to go forwards. Spiraling.

If the war on imagination is coiled through with paranoia – a desire-to-know entangled with a fear-of-regressing – then Fanon's findings further suggest that, as something between us and regression, it is the fear in fear-of-regressing to which psychologies might reflexively turn as a first step in waging war against the war on imagination. Chapter 4 describes how white ignorance traps us inside the colonial episteme while being haunted by a lingering sense of the violence and limits of this episteme, sending us in paranoid loops that, within psycurity, come to stabilize white supremacy. With Fanon's method, rather than desiring more knowledge, it is witnessing this lingering sense, feeling the feelings, that may help to break this cycle. Entering a fearful – not fearless – mode of perpetual discomfort that moves, struggles, unsettles. As Anzaldúa (1987) describes living with Coatlicue:

> Something pulsates in my body, a luminous thin thing that grows thicker every day. Its presence never leaves me. I am never alone.

That which abides: my vigilance, my thousand sleepless serpent eyes blinking in the night, forever open. And I am not afraid.

(Anzaldúa, 1987, p. 73)

I first cited this extract in Chapter 5's reparative reading of paranoia as beside-the-mind. This reading was driven by a lingering sense that the academic and activist praxis with which I was engaged was somehow violent and limited. That it tended toward not only lacking imagination, but being afraid of it. Doing a reparative reading required me to enter fears of being unscholarly, of being ignorant, of being complicit, of being white, of carrying on the genocidal legacy of my biological and intellectual ancestors. However, it was ultimately having these beings close-by that kept this project vigilant, lively, breathing. It was because of, not despite, these beings that the preceding chapters took their serpentine shape, both full of fear and unafraid. White blood cells slowly dripping out of the colonial episteme, losing a defensiveness against the irrational, the uncontrollable, the other, open to Césaire's (1941, 1943) "the strange, the marvellous, the fantastic" (as translated in Kelley, 1999, n.p.). An otherworldly correspondence, imagination.

For Fanon (1952), only the Negro has the capacity to convey and decipher this 'cosmic message.' However I wonder if prodromal experiences, likewise severed through coloniality, might also be able to teach something about this receptivity and translation, about a process of imagining whereby, as Anzaldúa (2002) describes, "all your antennae quiver and your body becomes a lightning rod, a radio receiver, a seismograph detecting and recording ground movement" (p. 292). Hearing the land with a more-than-human protrusion, sensing it with something that sticks out of the colonial epidermis, breaching the colonial episteme. Corresponding with another world. If so, the prodrome also enacts the 'open body' suggested by Maldonado-Torres (2016) as a fleshed anchor for decolonial critique; one that could lead to the emergence of 'an-other speech' and 'an-other thinking,' creating 'an-other knowledge' and 'an-other archive.' And thus offering psychologies an extra-ordinary strategy for combating the war on imagination: to not fit lives into pre-existing categories, but to make "new meanings, new concepts, and new forms of being human" (p. 16). Remembering that these meanings, concepts, and forms may not be so 'new' after all, and that the mad subject is not the only embodied subject in Psychology, not the only human open to re-creation.

Weaponless

As previously legitimated centers unravel from within, cityscapes degenerate, consciousness and identity splinter, the revolutionary subject who rises from the rubble is mutant: citizen subject of a new postmodern colonialism – and de-colonialism – active all at once.

(Sandoval, 2000, p. 36)

Chela Sandoval (2000) draws on US Third World feminisms to document how anti-supremacist social movement requires a mode of consciousness committed to a process of metamorphosis; a 'dance' well known by Indigenous and oppressed peoples skilled at resisting, manipulating, side-stepping neo/colonial states (Harris, 2007). Sandoval (2000) briefly calls these revolutionary, dancing subjects, these "new kinds of warriors" (p. 113), *shapeshifters*. Shapeshifters' power comes from an insistence on affinities through difference, allowing for "the guided use of any tool at one's disposal in order to ensure survival and to remake the world" (p. 171). Too slippery for colonization's grip, this shapeshifting defies categorization, breaching borders. Including, once again, between the neocolonial and the decolonial.

Anzaldúa's la facultad – from which I theorized beside-the-mind in Chapter 5 – is an inner technology of these shapeshifters, permitting one "to see, hear, and interpret what appeared natural to the colonizer as the cultural and historical productions they were" (p. 82). However, beside-the-mind suggests that this survival capacity is not just about denaturalizing coloniality; it is about engaging in otherworldly correspondence. One that, as per Chapter 6, is welcomed through mystery, ritual, and pausing – a tactic of magical ideation that both composts and enchants our psycuritized, suffocating soil, making space for imagination, for an otherworldly correspondence. Sandoval proposes that a 'methodology of the oppressed' is one that comprises techniques for moving energy, making up a field of force that drives, inspires, and focuses decolonizing ways of being and doing. She names the energy that is being moved by such a methodology, that accesses and guides these revolutionary maneuvers, *love*. And her project is to identify how this love is rising up in different forms, trespassing disciplinary borders, breaking 'academic apartheid.' The trick is thus for her, for us, to be able to recognize it, to be receptive to it, to follow it, to learn from it. I did not encounter Sandoval until after I had finished the first draft of this book. As a shapeshifting force that drives a space-making for otherworldly correspondence, the love that she identifies and articulates appears to have potentially risen up in my own text as magic. Suggesting that, as a collective of techniques for moving this magic, magical ideation may itself have the potential to be a methodology of the oppressed.[7]

Indeed Césaire (1941, 1943) herself writes of the abovementioned "magic power" that nourishes the "massive army of refusals" as emerging in "the metamorphoses and the inversions of the world under the sign of hallucination and madness" (as translated in Kelley, 1999, n.p.). However, Sandoval (2000) is resolute that moving love, moving magic, requires both psychic and activist techniques. In Chapter 2, I refer to an imperative to describe the mechanics of our contemporary control society, a serpent, in order to find out what we are being "made to serve" and to "look for new weapons" (Deleuze, 1992, p. 4). The undulating coils of this book – its content and form – suggest that what is demanding servitude within the neocolonial security state is otherworldly correspondence. With Sandoval (2000), this includes an accountability to bodies that know an-other world is not only possible but necessary – including the black, Indigenous, and immigrant justice movements that are currently shaking US white supremacy.

Through its Latin derivation, *radix*, 'root' connects the 'rhizome' with the 'radical.' For Stengers (2012) the metamorphic efficacy of magic depends on magical crafts being a rhizomatic operation – eternally connecting with other magical crafts – such that any attempts to revive Psychology's radical potential need to not only re-turn its roots but also be a collective maneuver. That is, breaching the borders of our discipline to join with those who can help us to not take things for granted, to withstand universalizing, to embody, to listen and learn. And to reciprocate. Silvia Federici (2014) documents how a battle against magic has always accompanied the development of capitalism, of coloniality. While the final sentence in her influential book calls for stripping this history of its "metaphysical trappings" in order to see how "close to home" it remains (p. 239), the preceding chapters suggest that these trappings might contribute to, not undermine, anti-capitalist, anti-colonial praxis. Emerging from a discipline both rooted in the study of psykhe and complicit in its capture and exile, psychologies have an ability, if not an obligation, to reclaim its radical value.

And so, a new weapon for psychologies committed to decoloniality may be to be "weaponless, standing with open arms, and only our magic" (Anzaldúa, 1987, p. 110). That is, to not stay in our pre-given worlds with only our usual weapons, but to enter the borderlands where weapons abound (Sandoval, 2000), finding the unfamiliar (Fanon, 1952), the strange, the marvelous, the fantastic (Cesaire, 1941, 1942, as translated in Kelley, 1999). Searching for seeds, not purity. And driven by a beside-the-mind sense that, unlike the paranoia offered by Eve Sedgwick (2003), brings a *mystified* approach to systemic oppressions. A radical praxis of healing, pedagogy, and protest premised on magical ideation, on making space for imagination, for correspondence with an-other world, here-now.

Diverging further and further from the normalizing grip of Psychology – in the singular and with a capital 'P' – perhaps this project has become more and more unsettling to it. Stretching the episteme for psychologies,

I hope that the preceding pages increase our surface area, our skin. Increasing our capacity to sense, widening our ability to respond to a twisted legacy of cosmological violence that continues to animate white supremacy. Reviving the psykhe of our studies and thus a response-ability in times of breathlessness.

Notes

1 This phrase is inspired by Frantz Fanon (1952) who briefly states that he will be "derelict" and refuse to put a method section at the beginning of his text because he considers psychological methods to ultimately "devour" themselves. Here, I have found this devouring to be a methodology in and of itself.
2 Indeed, the overall arc of this book first came through a poem, which was installed alongside a reprint of the 1907 Tohunga Suppression Act as part of *Missed Connections* in Tamaki Makaurau Auckland – described in Chapter 6 (see also Brigstocke & Noorani, 2017).
3 Robin Kelley (1999) suggests that Aimé Césaire's (1955) *Discourse on Colonialism* should be read as a surrealist text, Suzanne Césaire should be considered one of surrealism's "most original theorists," and that together the journal they edited from 1941 to 1945, *Tropiques,* became "one of the most important and radical surrealist publications in the world" (n.p.).
4 At el Jardín they speak of how Indigenous peoples used the color of cochineal in cosmetics, food, ink, dye, tribute, and local trade. When the Spanish arrived in the early sixteenth century, they coveted the bright red colors that cochineal produced, but were unable to cultivate it themselves given the bugs' insistence on the nopal cactuses and therefore their native land. Instead, the Spanish tried (and failed) to intensify its production with forced labor and passed law after law to ensure their monopoly over what was to become a global market for cochineal, with Oaxaca being the major area of production; in 1774, 700 tons of the bugs were shipped to Spain to color the church, the elite, and the military. This money was used to build Oaxaca into the city that it is today – the cochineal's stubbornness and color bought wealth to the region, protecting local peoples and cultures from complete coloniality. In the mid-nineteenth century, the production of synthetics in Europe replaced demand for the bugs, although Andean countries recaptured the market with natural dyes a century later. Continuing cochineal's legacy of coloring violent circuits of capital, one of its main importers became Starbucks – they used the bugs to color their strawberry Frappuccino until vegan protestors convinced them otherwise.
5 Initially, I struggled to make colors whose vibrancy lasted, accidentally realizing one day that the problem was the paper I was using. Finally, on November 30, 2016, on a day of protest against the privatization of education, when the city (and I) felt intensely agitated, I made seven cochineal presses on gloss paper. Seeing then that my previous attempts had also been fading in the light, I stored these ones in darkness, only bringing them out at night. The cochineal had forced me to draw by moonlight, reminding me about the importance of the milieu and the risks of (En)light(ened) pollution.
6 This drawing itself was an outsider praxis that I have been inadvertently developing over the past few years. Prefaced on repetition, emergence, and entanglement, I have in particular come to experience it as a means to learn

about shapeshifting – each 'mistake' works as a surprise, an unexpected and welcome intrusion that redirects the process, continually shifting the shape of the final image, opening up a correspondence.

7 This rising up of Chela Sandoval's (2000) 'love' appears to have happened in an environment made up of not only shared intellectual and political commitments (such as to border thinking and decoloniality), but other elements relating to Sandoval's methodology of the oppressed. Otherworldly correspondence resonates with her 'punctum,' making a passage to beside-the-mind, her 'abyss' – a borderland place of potential where political weapons abound; mystery/ritual/pausing are perhaps 'revolutionary maneuvers' because they are what are moved by and move the magic – Sandoval's 'love' – making a space, a 'field of force' for otherworldly correspondence, the punctum . . . Indeed my experience suggests that this methodology may be one that generates its energy by spiraling.

DRAWING 7. "Shapeshifting." Black ink on cochineal print, el Jardín Etnobotánico de Oaxaca. Rachel Jane Liebert, 2016.

REFERENCES

Adams, G., Dobles, I., Gomez, L., Kurtis, T., & Molina, L., (2015). Decolonizing psychological science: Introduction to the special thematic section. *Journal of Social and Political Psychology*, *3*(1): 213–238.
Addington, J., Cadenhead, K., Cannon, T., Cornblatt, B., McGlashan, T., Perkins, D., Seidman, L., Tsuang, M., Walker, E., Woods, S., & Heinssen, R. (2007). North American Prodrome Longitudinal Study: A collaborative multisite approach to prodromal schizophrenia research. *Schizophrenia Bulletin*, *33*(3): 665–672.
Addington, J., Cadenhead, K., Cornblatt, B., Mathalon, D., McGlashan, T., Perkins, D., Seidman, L., Tsuang, M., Walker, E., Woods, S., Addington, J.A., & Cannon, T. (2012). North American Prodrome Longitudinal Study (NAPLS 2): Overview and recruitment. *Schizophrenia Research*, *142*(1–3): 77–82.
Addington J., Liu L., Buchy L., Cadenhead K.S., Cannon T.D., Cornblatt B.A., Perkins D.O., Seidman L.J., Tsuang M.T., Walker E.F., Woods S.W., Bearden C.E., Mathalon D.H., & McGlashan T.H. (2015). North American Prodrome Longitudinal Study (NAPLS 2): The prodromal symptoms. *Journal of Nervous and Mental Disorders*, *203*: 328–335.
Ahmed, S. (2007). A phenomenology of whiteness. *Feminist Theory*, *8*(2): 149–168.
Alcoff, L. (1991). The problem of speaking for others. *Cultural Critique*, *20*: 5–32.
Alcoff, L. (2006). The whiteness question. Chapter in *Visible Identities: Race, Gender, and the Self*. New York: Oxford University Press.
Alcoff, L. (2007). Epistemologies of ignorance: Three types. In S. Sullivan & N. Tuana (Eds.), *Race and Epistemologies of Ignorance*. New York: SUNY Press.
Alexander, M. (2010). *The New Jim Crow: Mass Incarceration in the Age of Colorblindness*. New York: The New Press.
Anzaldúa, G. (no date). A short Q&A between LP and her author (GEA). In A. Keating (2009). *The Gloria Anzaldúa Reader*. Durham and London: Duke University Press.
Anzaldúa, G. (1986). Creativity and switching modes of consciousness. In A. Keating (2009). *The Gloria Anzaldúa Reader*. Durham and London: Duke University Press.

References

Anzaldúa, G. (1987) *Borderlands La Frontera: The New Mestiza*. San Francisco, CA: Aunt Lute Books.
Anzaldúa, G. (2001). (Un)natural bridges, (un)safe places. In A. Keating (2009). *The Gloria Anzaldúa Reader*. Durham and London: Duke University Press.
Anzaldúa, G. (2002). Speaking across the divide. In A. Keating (2009). *The Gloria Anzaldúa Reader*. Durham and London: Duke University Press.
APA (2013). *The Diagnostic and Statistical Manual of Mental Disorders, Fifth Edition (DSM-5)*. Arlington, VA: American Psychiatric Publishing.
Barad, K. (2007). *Meeting the Universe Halfway*. Durham and London: Duke University Press.
Barad, K. (2014) Diffracting diffraction: Cutting together-apart. *Parallax, 20*(3): 168–187.
Bayer, R. (1981). *Homosexuality and American Psychiatry: The Politics of Diagnosis*. New York: Basic Books.
Bhabha, H. (2004). Framing Fanon. In F. Fanon (1963). *The Wretched of the Earth*. Paris: Presence Africaine.
Bhatia, S. (2017). *Decolonizing Psychology: Globalizaton, Social Justice, and Indian Youth Identities*. Oxford University Press.
Biden, J. (2014, May 20). *Vice President Biden Addresses the APA Annual Meeting*. https://vimeo.com/94082947. Last accessed March 9, 2018.
Blackman, L. (2001). *Hearing Voices: Embodiment and Experience*. London: Free Association Press.
Blackman, L. (2010). Embodying affect: Voice-hearing, telepathy, suggestion and modelling the non-conscious. *Body & Society, 16*(1): 163–192.
Blackman, L. (2012). *Immaterial Bodies: Affect, Embodiment, Mediation*. London: SAGE.
Blackman, L. (2014). Immateriality, affectivity, experimentation: Queer science and future-psychology. *Transformations, 25*: 1–12.
Blackman, L., Cromby, J., Hook, D., Papadopoulos, D., & Walkerdine, V. (2008). Creating subjectivities. *Subjectivity, 22*: 1–27.
Blinder, A. & Sack, K. (2017, January 10). Dylann Roof is sentenced to death in Charleston church massacre. *New York Times*. www.nytimes.com/2017/01/10/us/dylann-roof-trial-charleston.html?_r=0. Last accessed March 9, 2018.
Brigstocke, J. & Noorani, T. (2017). *Listening with Non-Human Others*. Lewes: ARN Press. https://warwick.ac.uk/fac/soc/sociology/staff/blencowe/arn_press/listening_with_non-human_others_pdf.pdf. Last accessed March 9, 2018.
Bromberg, W. & Simon, F. (1968). The "protest" psychosis: A special type of reactive psychosis. *Archives of General Psychology, 19*(2): 155–160.
Brown, S., & Stenner, P. (2009). *Psychology Without Foundations: History, Philosophy, and Psychosocial Theory*. London: SAGE.
Browne-Marshall, G. (2013). Stop and frisk: From slave-catchers to NYPD, a legal commentary. *Trotter Review, 21*(1): Article 9.
Bush, G. (2002). President says US must make commitment to mental health care. Presidential remarks. University of New Mexico, Albuquerque, New Mexico. http://govinfo.library.unt.edu/mentalhealthcommission/20020429-1.htm. Last accessed February 16, 2018.
Butler, J. (1993). Endangered/endangering: Schematic racism and white paranoia. Chapter in R. Gooding-Williams (Ed.), *Reading Rodney King/Reading Urban Uprising*. New York and London: Routledge.

References

Candilis, P. (2003) Early intervention in schizophrenia: Three frameworks for guiding ethical inquiry. *Psychopharmacology*, 171(1): 75–80.

Cannon, T., Yu, C., Addington, J., Bearden, C., Cadenhead, K., Cornblatt, B., Heinssen, R., Jeffries, C., Mathalon, D., McGlashan, T., Perkins, D., Seidman, L., Tsuang, M., Walker, E., Woods, S., & Kattan, M. (2016). An individualized risk calculator for research in prodromal psychosis. *American Journal of Psychiatry*, 173(10): 980–988.

Carpenter, W.T. (2015). Attenuated psychosis syndrome: A new diagnostic class? *Journal of Nervous and Mental Disorders*, 203: 325–327.

Carpenter, W. & van Os, J. (2011). Should attenuated psychosis syndrome be a DSM-5 diagnosis? *The American Journal of Psychiatry*, 168(5): 460–463.

Cartwright, S. (1851). Report on the diseases and peculiarities of the Negro race. *De Bow's Review, Volume XI*.

Césaire, A. (1955). *Discourse on Colonialism*. Translated by J. Pinkham. New York: Monthly Review Press.

Chapman, L. & Chapman, J. (1980). Scales for rating psychotic and like experiences as continua. *Schizophrenia Bulletin*, 6: 476–489.

Chapman, L.J., Chapman, J.P., & Raulin, M.L. (1978). Body-image aberration in Schizophrenia. *Journal of Abnormal Psychology*, 87(4): 399.

Child Welfare (2015). Foster Care Statistics 2015. *Numbers and Trends, April*. Children's Bureau Child Welfare Information Gateway.

Clough, P. & Willse, C. (2010). Gendered security/national security: Political branding and population racism. *Social Text*, 28(4): 45–63.

Conrad, P. (1975). The discovery of hyperkinesis: Notes on the medicalization of deviant behavior. *Social Problems*, 23(1): 12–21.

Cromby, J., & Harper, D. (2012). Paranoia: Contested and contextualized. Chapter in B. Diamond, S. Coles, & S. Keenan (Eds.), Madness Contested: Power and Practice. Ross: PCCS Books.

Dabashi, H. (2015). *Can Non-Europeans Think?* London: Zed Books.

de Ávila, A. (2006). *La Espina y el Fruto: Jardín Etnobotanico de Oaxaca*. Mexico City: Artes de Mexico; Bilingual edition.

Deleuze, G. (1992). Postscript on the societies of control. *October*, 59(Winter): 3–7.

Deleuze, G. (1994). *Difference and Repetition*. Translated by P. Patton. New York: Columbia University Press.

Deleuze, G. & Guattari, F. (1972). *Anti-Oedipus: Capitalism and Schizophrenia*. Minneapolis, MN: University of Minnesota Press.

Deleuze, G. and Guattari, F. (1987) *A Thousand Plateaus: Capitalism and Schizophrenia*. Translated by B. Massumi. Minneapolis, MN: University of Minnesota Press.

Dickerson, F. (2015). Early detection and intervention for people with psychosis: Getting to the bottom line. *The Journal and Mental and Nervous Disease*, 203(5): 307–309.

DuBois, W.E.B. (1903). *The Souls of Black Folk*. Chicago, IL: A.C. McClurg Company.

Duncan (2016, December 7). Is Dylann Roof intentionally hiding his mental state? *Reveal: The Center for Investigative Reporting*. www.revealnews.org/blog/is-dylann-roof-intentionally-hiding-his-mental-state/. Last accessed March 9, 2018.

Eckblad, M. & Chapman, L. (1983) Magical ideation as an indicator of schizotypy. *Journal of Consulting and Clinical Psychology*, 51(2): 215–225.

References

Elder, H. (2015). Te waka oranga: Bringing indigenous knowledge forward. In K. McPherson, B.E. Gibson & A. Leplege (Eds.), *Rethinking Rehabilitation: Theory and Practice* (pp. 227–246). Boca Raton, Florida: CRC Press Taylor and Francis.

Falloon, I. (1992). Early intervention for first episodes of schizophrenia: A preliminary exploration. *Psychiatry*, 55: 4–15.

Fanon, F. (1952). *Black Skin, White Masks*. Paris: Editions du Seuil.

Fanon, F. (1963). *The Wretched of the Earth*. Paris: Presence Africaine.

FBI (2018). What we investigate: Hate crimes. www.fbi.gov/investigate/civil-rights/hate-crimes. Last accessed March 9, 2018.

Federici, S. (2014). *Caliban and the Witch: Women, the Body, and Primitive Accumulation*, 2nd Edition. New York: Autonomedia.

Fine, M. (2012). Troubling calls for evidence: A critical race, class and gender analysis of whose evidence counts. *Feminism & Psychology*, 22(1): 3–19.

Foucault (1983). Preface. In G. Deleuze & F. Guattari, *Anti-Oedipus: Capitalism and Schizophrenia*. Minneapolis, MN: University of Minnesota Press.

Fricker, M. (2008). Epistemic injustice: Power and the ethics of knowing (Precis). *Theoria*, 61: 69–71.

Frosh, S. (2016). Relationality in a time of surveillance: Narcissism, melancholia, paranoia. *Subjectivity*, 9(1): 1–16. http://eprints.bbk.ac.uk/13296/1/Narcissism%2C%20Melancholia%2C%20Paranoia%20Final.pdf Last accessed March 26, 2018.

Fusar-Poli, P., Bonoldi, I., Yung, A.R., Borgwardt, S., Kempton, M.J., Valmaggia, L., Barale, F., Caverzasi, E., & McGuire, P. (2012). Predicting psychosis: Meta-analysis of transition outcomes in individuals at high clinical risk. *Archives of General Psychiatry*, 69(3): 220–229.

Fusar-Poli, P., Borgwardt, S., Bechdolf, A., Addington, J., Riecher-Rossler, A., Schultze-Lutter, F., Keshavan, M., Wood, S., Ruhrmann, S., Seidman, L.J., Valmaggia, L., Cannon, T., Velthorst, E., De Haan, L., Cornblatt, B., Bonoldi, I., Birchwood, M., McGlashan, T., Carpenter, W., McGorry, P., Klosterkötter, J., McGuire, P., & Yung, A. (2013). The psychosis high-risk state: A comprehensive state-of-the-art review. *JAMA Psychiatry*, 70:107–120.

Fusar-Poli, P., Carpenter, W.T., Woods, S.W., McGlashan, T.H. (2014). Attenuated psychosis syndrome: Ready for DSM 5.1? *Annual Review of Clinical Psychology*, 10: 155–192.

Grewal, I. (2003). Transnational America: Race, gender, and citizenship after 9/11. *Social Identities*, 9(4): 535–561.

Goodchild, P. (1996). *Deleuze and Guattari: An Introduction to the Politics of Desire*. London: SAGE.

Hage, G. (2003). Multiculturalism and white paranoia in Australia. *JIMI/RIMI*, 3(3–4): 417–437.

Harper, D. (2008). The politics of paranoia: Paranoid positioning and conspirational narratives in the surveillance society. *Surveillance & Society*, 5(1): 1–32.

Harris, A. (2007). *Dancing with the State: Māori Creative Energy and Policies of Integration, 1945–1967*. PhD Thesis, History: University of Auckland.

Harvey, D. (2007). *A Brief History of Neoliberalism*. New York: Oxford University Press.

References

Heinssen, R. (2015, Feb 6). Early Psychosis Intervention Network (EPINET): A Learning Healthcare System for Early Serious Mental Illness. *NAMHC Concept Clearance*. Accessed August 19, 2018: www.nimh.nih.gov/funding/grant-writing-and-application-process/concept-clearances/2015/early-psychosis-intervention-network-epinet-a-learning-healthcare-system-for-early-serious-mental-illness.shtml

Hemmings, C. (2005). Invoking affect: Cultural theory and the ontological turn. *Cultural Studies*, *19*(5): 548–567.

Hillman, J. (1975). *Re-visioning Psychology*. New York: Harper & Row.

Hook, D. (2012). *A Critical Psychology of the Postcolonial: The Mind of the Apartheid*. London and New York: Psychology Press.

Jordan, W. (1968). *White Over Black: American Attitudes Toward the Negro, 1550–1812*. Chapel Hill, NC: The University of North Carolina Press.

Jones, P. (2017). Is early intervention research stuck in its psychosis prediction paradigm? *IEPA: Early Intervention in Mental Health*. https://iepa.org.au/is-early-intervention-research-stuck-in-its-psychosis-prediction-paradigm/. Last accessed March 9, 2018.

Jung, C.G. (1931) Archaic man. *The Collected Works of CG Jung*, 10: 104–147.

Kamens, S., Elkins, D., & Robbins, B. (2017). Open letter to the DSM-5. *Journal of Humanistic Psychology*, *57*(6): 675–687.

Katz, C. (2007) Banal terrorism: Spatial fetishism and everyday insecurity. In D. Gregory & A. Pred (Eds), *Violent Geography. Fear, Terror, and Political Violence*. New York: Routledge.

Keating, A. (2009). *The Gloria Anzaldúa Reader*. Durham and London: Duke University Press.

Kelley, R. (1999, November). A poetics of anticolonialism. *Monthly Review*, *51*(6). https://monthlyreview.org/1999/11/01/a-poetics-of-anticolonialism/. Last accessed March 9, 2018.

Kelley, R. (2000). A poetics of anticolonialism. In A. Cesaire (1955), *Discourse on Colonialism*. Translated by J. Pinkham. New York: Monthly Review Press.

KFF (2016). Medicaid enrolment by race/ethnicity. *State Health Facts*. The Henry J. Kaiser Family Foundation. http://kff.org/medicaid/state-indicator/medicaid-enrollment-by-raceethnicity/. Last accessed March 9, 2018.

Latour, B. (2011) Foreword. In I. Stengers, *Thinking With Whitehead: A Free and Wild Creation of Ideas*. Boston, MA: Harvard Press.

Levinson (2015). Second generation antipsychotic drug use among Medicaid enrolled children: Quality of care concern. Department of Health and Human Services Office of Inspector General, March. http://oig.hhs.gov/oei/reports/oei-07-12-00320.pdf. Last accessed March 9, 2018.

Levy-Bruhl, L. (1985 [1926]) *How Natives Think* [1910 in French]. Translated by L.A. Clare. Princeton, NJ: Princeton University Press.

Liebert, R. (2010). Synaptic peace-keeping: Of bipolar and securitization. *Women's Studies Quarterly Special Issue, Market*, *38*(3&4): 325–342.

Liebert, R. (2013a). Loopy: The political ontology of Bipolar Disorder. *Aporia*, *5*(3): 15–25.

Liebert, R. (2013b). A progressive downward spiral: The circulation of risk in 'bipolar disorder'. *Journal of Theoretical and Philosophical Psychology*, *33*(3): 185–198.

Liebert, R. (2014). Psy policing: The borderlands of psychiatry and security. In D. Holmes, J.D. Jacob, & A. Perron (Eds.), *Power and the Psychiatric Apparatus: Repression, Transformation and Assistance*. Farnham, Surrey: Ashgate.

Liebert, R.J. (2017a). Beside-the-mind: An unsettling, reparative reading of paranoia. *Subjectivity*, *10*(1): 123–145.

Liebert, R. (2017b). Radical archiving as social psychology from the future. *Qualitative Psychology Special Issue, The Archive*, *4*: 90.

Liebert, R. & Gavey, N. (2009). "There's always two sides to these things": Managing the dilemmas of serious adverse effects from SSRI use. *Social Science and Medicine*, *68*(10): 1882–1891.

Lorde, A. (1984). *Sister Outsider*. New York: Crossing Press.

Lugones, M. (2010). Toward a decolonial feminism. *Hypatia*, *25*(4): 742–759.

Maldonado-Torres, N. (2006). Cesaire's gift and the decolonial turn. *Radical Philosophy Review*, *9*(2): 111–138.

Maldonado-Torres, N. (2016). *Outline of Ten Theses on Coloniality and Decoloniality*. Frantz Fanon Foundation. http://frantzfanonfoundation-fondationfrantzfanon.com/IMG/pdf/maldonado-torres_outline_of_ten_theses-10.23.16_.pdf. Last accessed March 9, 2018.

Marcel, G. (1995). *The Philosophy of Existentialism*. Translated by M. Harari. New York: Carol Publishing Group.

Martín-Baro, I. (1994). *Writings for a Liberation Psychology*. Cambridge, MA: Harvard University Press.

Massumi, B. (2005). Fear (the spectrum said). *Positions*, *13*(1): 31–48.

Massumi, B. (2010) The future birth of the affective fact: The political ontology of threat. In M. Gregg & G. Seigworth (Eds.), *The Affect Theory Reader*. London: Duke University Press.

Massumi, B. (2015). *Politics of Affect*. Cambridge: Polity Press.

McGlashan, T. (2015). From treating to preventing psychosis. *Journal of Nervous and Mental Disease*, *203*(5): 352–355.

McGlashan, T., Miller, T., & Woods, S. (2001). Pre-onset detection and intervention research in schizophrenia psychosis: Current estimates of benefit and risk. *Schizophrenia Bulletin*, *27*(4): 563–570.

McGorry, P.D. (2015). Early intervention in psychosis: Obvious, effective, overdue. *Journal of Nervous and Mental Disease*, *203*(5): 310–318.

McManus, S. (2011). Hope, fear, and the politics of affective agency. *Theory and Event*, *14*(4).

Memmi, A. (1957, 1991). *The Colonizer and the Colonized*. Boston, MA: Beacon.

Metzl, J. (2009). *The Protest Psychosis: How Schizophrenia Became a Black Disease*. Boston, MA: Beacon Press.

Mignolo, W.D. (2012). *Local Histories/Global Designs: Coloniality, Subaltern Knowledges, and Border Thinking*. Princeton, NJ: Princeton University Press.

Mignolo, W. & Vázquez, R. (2013). Decolonial AestheSis: Colonial Wounds/Decolonial Healings. *Social Text Online*. https://socialtextjournal.org/periscope_article/decolonial-aesthesis-colonial-woundsdecolonial-healings/. Last accessed March 9, 2018.

Miller, G. (2018). Madness decolonized? Madness as transnational identity in Gail Hornstein's Agnes's Jacket. *Journal of Medical Humanities*, *39*(3): 303–323.

References

Miller, J.H. (1977). The critic as host. *Critical Inquiry*, *3*(3): 439–447.

Miller, T., McGlashan, T., Woods, S., Stein, K., Driesen, N., Corcoran, C., Hoffman, R., & Davidson, L. (1999). Symptom assessment in schizophrenic prodromal states. *Psychiatric Quarterly*, *70*(4): 273–287.

Miller, T.J., McGlashan, T.H., Rosen, J.L., Somjee, L., Marcovich, P.J., Stein, K., & Woods, S.W. (2002). Prospective diagnosis of the initial prodrome for schizophrenia based on the structured interview for prodromal syndromes: Preliminary evidence of interrater reliability and predictive validity. *American Journal of Psychiatry*, *159*: 863–865.

Mills, C. (2007). White ignorance. In S. Sullivan & N. Tuana (Eds.), *Race and Epistemologies of Ignorance*. New York: SUNY Press.

Mohanty, C.T. (2003) *Feminism Without Borders: Decolonizing Theory, Practicing Solidarity*. Durham and London: Duke University Press.

Moynihan, R. & Cassels, A. (2005). *Selling Sickness: How the World's Biggest Pharmaceutical Companies are Turning Us All into Patients*. New York: Nation Books.

Myers, N. (2015). Conversations on plant sensing: Notes from the field. *NatureCulture*, *3*: 35–66.

Nathan, T. (1999). *Georges Devereux and Clinical Ethnopsychiatry*, Translated by C. Grandsard. Paris: Centre Georges Devereux. www.ethnopsychiatrie.net/GDengl.htm. Last accessed March 9, 2018.

National Council for Community Behavioral Healthcare (2013). USA mental health first aid, 2008–2013 in review. *National Council Magazine, 1*.

National Public Radio (NPR; 2013, Feb 9). Despite shadow of Sandy Hook, schools considered 'safe'. *Weekend Edition Saturday*. www.npr.org/2013/02/09/171554782/despite-shadow-of-sandy-hook-schools-are-a-safe-place. Last accessed March 9, 2018.

Nelson, B. (2014) Attenuated psychosis syndrome: Don't jump the gun. *Psychopathology*, *47*: 292–296.

NIMH (1999). Prevention and early intervention in psychotic disorders. *PA, National Institute of Mental Health*. https://grants.nih.gov/grants/guide/pa-files/PA-99-090.html. Last accessed March 9, 2018.

NYT (2016, December 9). The Dylann Roof trial: The evidence. *The New York Times*. www.nytimes.com/interactive/2016/12/09/us/dylann-roof-evidence.html. Last accessed December 14, 2016.

Oliver, K. (2004). *The Colonization of Psychic Space: A Psychoanalytic Social Theory of Oppression*. Minneapolis, MN: The University of Minnesota Press.

Olsen, K. & Rosenbaum, B. (2006). Prospective investigations of the prodromal state of schizophrenia: Review of studies. *Acta Psychiatr Scand*, *113*: 247–272.

Patton, P. (2000). *Deleuze and the Political*. Routledge: New York.

Piers Morgan Tonight Show (2012). Inside the mind of a killer. *CNN*. http://edition.cnn.com/videos/bestoftv/2012/12/18/pmt-ct-shooting-dr-mehmet-oz-dr-michael-welner.cnn. Last accessed March 9, 2018.

Pies, R. (2015, February 2). Campus protests, narcissism, and the dearth of civility. *Psychiatric Times*. http://behaviorismandmentalhealth.com/wp-content/uploads/2016/01/Psychiatric_Times_-_Campus_Protests_Narcissism_and_the_Dearth_of_Civility_-_2015-12-03-2.pdf. Last accessed March 9, 2018.

References

Pignarre, P. & Stengers, I. (2011). *Capitalist Sorcery: Breaking the Spell*. Translated by A. Goffey. London: Palgrave MacMillan.

Pillay, S. (2017). Cracking the fortress: Can we really decolonize psychology? *South African Journal of Psychology*, *47*(2): 135–140.

Pillow, W. (2003). Confession, catharsis, or cure? Rethinking the uses of reflexivity as methodological power in qualitative research.*International Journal of Qualitative Studies in Education*,*16*(2), 175–196.

Protevi, J. (2009). *Political Affect: Connecting the Social and the Somatic*. Minneapolis: The University of Minnesota Press.

Puar, J. (2007). *Terrorist Assemblages: Homonationalism in Queer Times*. Durham and London: Duke University Press.

Puar, J. & Rai, A. (2002). Monster, terrorist, fag: The war on terrorism and the production of docile patriots. *Social Text*, *20*(3): 117–148.

Randazzo, M., & Cameron, K. (2012). From presidential protection to campus security: A brief history of threat assessment in North American Schools and Colleges. *Journal of College Student Psychotherapy*, *26*: 277–290.

Reiss, B. (2010). Madness after Virginia Tech. *Social Text*, *28* (4): 25–44.

Robles, F. (2015, June 20). Dylann Roof photos and a manifesto are posted on website. *New York Times*. www.nytimes.com/2015/06/21/us/dylann-storm-roof-photos-website-charleston-church-shooting.html?mtrref=www.google.co.uk&gwh=B611AC53B88F75713FE62C758314F0D7&gwt=pay&assetType=nyt_now. Last accessed March 9, 2018.

Robles, F., Horowitz, J., & Dewan, S. (2015, June 18). Dylann Roof, suspect in Charleston shooting, flew the flags of white power. *New York Times*. www.nytimes.com/2015/06/19/us/on-facebook-dylann-roof-charleston-suspect-wears-symbols-of-white-supremacy.html. Last accessed March 9, 2018.

Robles, F. & Stewart, N. (2015, July 16). Dylann Roof's Past reveals trouble at home and school. *New York Times*. www.nytimes.com/2015/07/17/us/charleston-shooting-dylann-roof-troubled-past.html?_r=0. Last accessed March 9, 2018.

Rose, N. (2010). Screen and intervene: Governing risky brains. *History of the Human Sciences*, *23*: 79–105.

Rowe, A.C. & Tuck, E. (2017). Settler colonialism and cultural studies: Ongoing settlement, cultural production, and resistance. *Cultural Studies* ⇔ *Critical Methodologies*, June: 1–11.

Roy, D. (2016). Neuroscience and feminist theory: A new directions essay. *Signs: Journal of Women and Culture in Society*, *41*(3): 531–552.

Rubin, D.M., Matone, H., Huang, Y.S., dosReis, S., Feudtner, C., & Localio, R. (2012) Interstate variation in trends of psychotropic medication use among Medicaid-enrolled children in foster care. *Children and Youth Services Review*, 34(8): 1492–1499.

Sack, K. (2016, November 28). Dylann Roof to represent himself at trial in Charleston church shootings. *New York Times*. www.nytimes.com/2016/11/28/us/dylann-roof-charleston-massacre.html. Last accessed March 9, 2018.

Sack, K. (2017, February 2). Trial documents show Dylann Roof had mental disorders. *New York Times*. www.nytimes.com/2017/02/02/us/dylann-roof-charleston-killing-mental.html. Last accessed March 9, 2018.

References

Sack, K., & Binder, A. (2016, December 9). Jurors hear Dylann Roof explain shooting in video: 'I had to do it'. *New York Times*. www.nytimes.com/2016/12/09/us/dylann-roof-shooting-charleston-south-carolina-church-video.html. Last accessed March 9, 2018.

Sandoval, C. (2000). *Methodology of the Oppressed*. Minneapolis, MN: University of Minnesota Press.

Seddon, T. (2010). Dangerous liaisons: Personality disorder and the politics of risk. *Punishment & Society, 10*: 301–317.

Sedgwick, E. (2003) *Touching Feeling: Affect, Pedagogy, Performativity*. Berkeley, CA: Duke University Press.

Segal, R. (2007) Jung and Levy-Bruhl. *Journal of Analytical Psychology, 52*: 635–658.

Segalo, P. Manoff, E., & Fine, M. (2015). Working with embroideries and counter-maps: Engaging memory and imagination within decolonizing frameworks. *Journal of Social and Political Psychology, 3*(1): 342–384.

Shalett, K. (2013, January 25). Aspen homeland security group prepares to advise Secretary Napolitano on gun violence in the wake of Newtown. *The Aspen Idea Blog*. www.aspeninstitute.org/about/blog/aspen-homeland-security-group-prepares-advise-secretary-napolitano-gun-violence-wake. Last accessed March 9, 2018.

Shamas, D. & Arastu, N. (2015). *Mapping Muslims: NYPD Spying and its Impact on American Muslims*. Report for Muslim American Civil Liberties Coalition (MACLC), Creating Law Enforcement Accountability & Responsibility (CLEAR) Project, & Asian American Legal Defense and Education Fund (AALDEF). www.law.cuny.edu/academics/clinics/immigration/clear/Mapping-Muslims.pdf. Last accessed March 9, 2018.

Sharma, A. (2009). Postcolonial racism: White paranoia and the terrors of multiculturalism. In G. Huggan and I. Law (Eds.), *Racism Postcolonialism Europe*. Liverpool: Liverpool University Press.

Sharma, S. & Sharma, A. (2003). White paranoia: Orientalism in the age of empire. *Fashion Theory, 7*(3–4): 301–317.

Smith, A. (2012). Indigeneity, settler colonialism, white supremacy. Chapter in D. HoSang, O. LaBennett, & L. Pulido (Eds.), *Racial Formation in the Twenty-First Century*. Berkeley, CA: University of California Press.

Spivak, G. (1988) Can the subaltern speak? In C. Nelson and L. Grossberg (Eds.), *Marxism and the Interpretation of Culture*. Basingstoke: Macmillan Education.

SPLC (2015, November 1). Terror from the right. Southern Poverty Law Center. www.splcenter.org/20151101/terror-right. Last accessed March 9, 2018.

Srihari, V.H., Tek, C., Pollard, J., Zimmet, S., Keat, J., Cahill, J.D., Kucukgoncu, S., Walsh, B.C., Li, F., Gueorguieva, R., Levine, N., Mesholam-Gately, R.I., Friedman-Yakoobian, M., Seidman, L.J., Keshavan, M.S., McGlashan, T.H., & Woods, S.W. (2014). Reducing the duration of untreated psychosis and its impact in the U.S.: The STEP-ED study. *BMC Psychiatry, 14*: 335.

Stengers, I. (2011) *Thinking with Whitehead: A Free and Wild Creation of Ideas*. Boston, MA: Harvard Press.

Stengers, I. (2012). Reclaiming animism. *e-flux Journal, 36*(July): 1–10.

Stewart-Harawira, M. (2005). *The New Imperial Order: Indigenous Responses to Globalization*. Wellington, New Zealand: Zed Books.

Szasz, T. (1960). The myth of mental illness. *American Psychologist, 15*: 113–118.
Taitimu, M., Read, J., & McIntosh, T. (2018). Nga Whakawhitinga (standing at the crossroads): How Maori understand what Western psychiatry calls 'schizophrenia'. *Transcultural Psychiatry, 0*(0): 1–25.
Teo, T. (2010). What is epistemological violence in the empirical social sciences? *Social and Personality Psychology Compass, 4*(5): 295–303.
Tiefer, L. (2006). Female sexual dysfunction: A case study of disease mongering and activist resistance. *PLoS Medicine, 3*(4): e178.
Todd, Z. (2016). An Indigenous feminist's take on the ontological turn: 'Ontology' is just another word for colonialism. *Journal of Historical Sociology, 29*(1): 4–22.
Trinh, M. (1989). *Woman, Native, Other: Writing Postcoloniality and Feminism.* Bloomington and Indianapolis: Indiana University Press.
Tuck, E., & McKenzie, M. (2015). Relational validity and the "where" of inquiry: Place and land in qualitative research. *Qualitative Inquiry, 21*(7): 633–638.
Tuck, E. & Yang, W. (2012) Decolonization is not a metaphor. *Decolonization: Indigeneity, Education & Society, 1*(1): 1–40.
Tuhiwai Smith, L. (1999). *Decolonizing Methodologies: Research and Indigenous Peoples.* London: Zed Books.
US Government Accountability Office (2017, April). Countering violent extremism: Actions needed to define strategy and assess progress of federal efforts. *Report to Congressional Requestors.* United States Government Accountability Office. /www.gao.gov/assets/690/683984.pdf. Last accessed March 9, 2018.
Ussher, J. (1991). *Women's Madness: Misogyny or Mental Illness?* New York: Harvester Wheatsheaf.
van Os, J., & Guloksuz, S. (2017). A critique of the 'ultra-high risk' and 'transition' paradigm. *World Psychiatry, 16*: 200–206.
Veracini, L. (2011). Introducing. *Settler Colonial Studies, 1*(1): 1–12.
Voyce, M. (1989) Māori healers in New Zealand: The Tohunga Suppression Act 1907. *Oceania, 60*(2): 99–123.
Watkins, M. & Shulman, H. (2008). *Toward Psychologies of Liberation.* New York: Palgrave MacMillan.
Whiteford, H., Ferrari, A., Degenhardt, L., Feigin, V., & Vos, T. (2015). The global burden of mental, neurological and substance use disorders: An analysis from the Global Burden of Disease Study 2010. *PLoS One, 10*(2): e0116820.
Whitehead, A.N. (1920). *The Concept of Nature.* Cambridge: Cambridge University Press.
Woodard, W. (2014) Politics, psychotherapy, and the 1907 Tohunga Suppression Act. *Psychotherapy and Politics International, 12*(1): 39–48.
Woods, S., Miller, T., & McGlashan, T. (2001). The "prodromal" patient: Both symptomatic and at-risk. *CNS Spectrum, 6*(3): 223–232.
Woods, S., Walsh, B., Saksa, J., & McGlashan, T. (2010). The case for including attenuated psychotic symptoms syndrome in DSM-5 as a psychosis risk syndrome. *Schizophrenia Research, 123*(2–3): 199–207.
Wynter, Sylvia (2003). Unsettling the coloniality of being/power/truth/freedom: Towards the human. *The New Centennial Review, 3*(3): 257–337.

Yung, A. (2003). Commentary: The schizophrenia prodrome: A high-risk concept. *Schizophrenia Bulletin, 29*(4): 859–865.

Yung, A. (2017). Treatment of people at ultra-high risk for psychosis. *World Psychiatry, 16*(20): 207–208.

Zamani, N. (2015). Race and Criminal Justice in the United States. *Statement of the Center for Constitutional Rights: Hearing before the InterAmerican Commission on Human Rights.* www.ccrjustice.org/sites/default/files/assets/files/CCR_IACHR_RaceCJ_Testimony20150316Final.pdf. Last accessed March 9, 2018.

INDEX

activism 85, 93, 138–140; black 2, 5, 32–33, 34–35, 89–90, 92; and imagination 127–128, 135–140; Indigenous 7, 134; and paranoia 8, 10–11, 96–97, 113, 135, 139; *see also* schools/and protests
aesthesis 117; *see also* art/as collaborator; *see also* breathing; *see also* decoloniality/through feeling; *see also* decoloniality/through form; *see also* discomfort; *see also* sensing
Anzaldúa, Gloria: *see also* border/and borderlands; and ignorance 80; *see also* Coatlicue; and la facultad 103, 138; and imagination 121, 123–124, 125, 131–133, 136–137; and response-ability 3–4, 6; and serpents 97–99; and weaponlessness 138–140
apprenticeship 116–118
art: as collaborator 117–118, 119–127, 132–134; as decolonising 8, 115–116, 117, 126; drawings 16, 39, 76, 95, 114, 129, 132–134, 142; public central plate, 118–127; with Science 8, 115–116; *see also* surrealism

Barad, Karen: and agential realism 97, 118–119, 127; and diffraction 106–107, 110–111; and re-turning 112, 115–116, 118–127
beside-the-mind: as method 10, 97, 118, 122; and imagination 130, 136–137, 138; and paranoia 99, 111–113, 139
blood 1–8; and bleeding 6, 95, 135–136; as lube 4
border 80, 89, 100; and borderguards 11, 50–60, 77; and borderlands 3, 104–107, 111–113, 119, 131, 132–133; and thinking 10–11, 99–107, 122, 131–132; breaching the 121–122, 124, 126, 131–132, 138–139
breach: *see* border/breaching the; *see* episteme/breaching the
breathing: 114, 115, 119–128; and activism 7, 127–128, 130–13, 135–137, 140; space 124–127; and breathlessness 4–5, 7–8, 118, 127, 136, 140; fresh air 7, 127–128; through magical ideation 127–128, 130–131; through mystery 120–122; as imagination 135–137; through pausing 124–127; and paranoia 93, 115; and Psychology 8, 113, 118, 120, 135–137, 140; through ritual 122–124

Césaire, Suzanne 6, 132, 134–135, 138–139
Coatlicue 93, 101–113, 116–117, 130, 131, 136–137
cochineal: *see* art/drawings
coloniality 3, 134; *see also* breathing/breathlessness; and colonisation 1–2;

Index

and decoloniality 119, 126, 137–138; and dehumanization 78, 135; and de-supernaturalization 7–8, 78, 109–110, 115, 135, 139; and gender 6–7, 78–79; and desire-to-know 78–79; and fear-of-regressing 80–83; and ignorance 79–80, 131; and paranoia 9, 83–85; and Psychology 9–11, 35, 79, 107–111, 131; trapped in 3–6, 9–10; *see also* white supremacy

control society 35–36, 73, 77, 85–93; *see also* serpent

cracks: *see also* art/drawings; and imagination 11, 107, 112, 125–126, 132–134; and the prodrome 46; in white supremacy 84–86, 91–93, 130, 134–135

decoloniality: *see also* aesthesis; *see also* border/thinking; *see also* breach; *see also* breathing; and coloniality 119, 126, 137–138; *see also* discomfort; through feeling 135–137; and feminism 6–7; through form 3–4, 9–11, 115–116, 120–128, 131–134; and imagination 110, 130–131, 134–137; and madness 9, 11, 137; and magical ideation 127–128, 130–131, 137–139; and paranoia 80–85; through questioning 5, 117, 122; *see also* reflexivity; solidarity with 3–4, 11, 137–139; *see also* surrealism

discomfort 3–8, 98–99, 122, 128, 134, 136; as unsettling 9, 85, 91, 112, 139–140

dis-ease: *see* discomfort; *see* paranoia/as dis-ease

episteme: beside the 10, 122, 130; breaching the 4–5, 6, 14, 112, 118, 137–140; trapped in the 4–5, 6, 10, 80, 91, 135–136

experimenting 8, 11, 96, 116–118, 121–122, 133

Fanon, Frantz: and whiteness 3–8, 80–82; and method 4, 9, 115, 122, 131n1, 132, 135–137; and reason 8, 86; and worldliness 109

fear: and hyper-saturated solution 8, 32, 60, 90, 91–92, 111; as method 119, 135–137; and paranoia 83–92, 130; of 'regressing' 80–83, 110

flesh: and coloniality 78–79; as method 3–6, 106, 124, 128, 131, 135–137

imagination: *see* otherworldly correspondence

Indigeneity: *see also* activism/Indigenous; *see also* Coatlicue; erasure of 2, 78–79, 101n2, 118n1; *see also* Tohunga Suppression Act

infernal alternative 41–42, 51, 60, 73, 97, 100; and ignorance 82

love 135–137

magic 81, 108–111, 121, 123–124, 126, 139; magic bullet 67–68; *see also* magical ideation; as method 127, 135–137; *see also* witches

magical ideation: art central plate, 118–119, 120, 123, 125; scale 101, 110, 116–117; as method 127–128, 132–134, 136–139

Missed Connections 111; *see also* art/public

more-than-human: *see also* Coatlicue; and de-supernaturalization 7–8, 78, 109–110, 115, 135, 139; *see also* otherworldly correspondence/as more-than-human; and method 99, 111–113, 115–118, 119–127, 131–134, 135–137; *see also* plants; *see also* serpent; *see also* worms

mystery 3, 120–122, 127–128, 131–134

neocolonial security state 2–3, 8–9, 31–36, 106–111, 127–128; *see also* psycurity; *see also* otherworldly correspondence/war on imagination

normal: *see* infernal alternative

ontologic injustice 107–111

otherworldly correspondence: 115–116; 130–134; *see also* activism/and imagination; *see also* Anzaldúa/and imagination; *see also* beside-the-mind/and imagination; *see also* breathing/as imagination; *see also* cracks/and imagination; *see also* decoloniality/and imagination; imaginative leap 103–104, 112–113, 116; and magic 121,

156 Index

123–124, 126, 127; making space for 115–116, 119–127, 127–128; as method 131–137; as more-than-human 101–104, 104–107, 107–111, 131–134, 135–137, 119–127; as paranoia's roots 104–107, 119, 130; and prodrome 55, 99–101, 101–104, 104–107; and Psychology 128–129, 122, 124, 127, 135–136, 137–139; war on imagination 134–137

paranoia: *see also* activism/and paranoia; *see also* beside-the-mind/and paranoia; as dis-ease 5, 8–9, 10, 23, 83–85, 91; *see also* otherworldly correspondence/as paranoia's roots; paranoid reading 93, 96; *see also* psycurity; *see also* reparative reading
pausing 124–127, 127–128, 131–134
plants 16, 39, 76, 95, 114, 129, 132–134, 142
pharma 26, 33, 66–67, 68; and antipsychotics 24, 26, 32, 65, 67–68; and disease-mongering 32n21, 33, 48, 88–89
policing 8–9, 11, 32–33, 80, 83–84, 91–92; *see also* neocolonial security state; *see also* surveillance
prodrome 23–28, 40–41; as assemblage 77; *see also control society*; DSM 26–27; *see also* otherworldly correspondence/and prodrome; instruments for diagnosing the 24, 50–60; *see also* magical ideation; and psychosis 61–66; *see also* psycurity; recruitment of 42–50; *see also* reparative reading; studies of 67–73
psycurity 85–93; *see also* otherworldly correspondence/war on imagination
Psychology: *see also* breathing/and Psychology; comfort zone of 9, 48, 98–99, 122, 131–134, 139–140; *see also* coloniality/and Psychology; *see also* discomfort; *see also* response-ability; *see also* otherworldly correspondence/war on imagination
psykhe: *see* breathing

Rangiaowhia 1–2, 7
reflexivity: *see also* art/as collaborator; *see also* discomfort; of settler ancestry 1–8, 134, 137; of white skin 4–6, 137; of white women 6–8
reparative reading 10–11, 96–97, 111–113, 139
response-ability 3–4, 11, 139–140; *see also* decoloniality/solidarity with; *see also* otherworldly correspondence/making space for; *see also* magical ideation/as method; *see also* reflexivity; *see also* reparative reading; *see also* sensing
ritual 122–124, 127–128, 131–134

Sandoval, Chela 10n10, 91; methodology of the oppressed 137–139, 138n7
Schizophrenia: and blackness 32–33; *see also* prodrome; and protest 32–33
schools: and Sandy Hook shooting 28–31, 43, 46–47, 73, 90; and Threat Assessment 34; and Virginia Tech shooting 34; and the prodrome 42–50; and protests 34–35
seeping 76, 85, 93, 130, 135
sensing 16; *see also* beside-the-mind; as method 5–6, 42n2; and prodrome 57–58, 97, 103; and paranoia 81, 83–85, 91; and revolution 14, 134, 135–137, 139–140
serpent 35–36, 77, 85–90, 93, 97–104, 131, 139
spiraling 129; as method 5, 119–127, 131, 132–132, 134; and *paranoia* 23, 80, 83, 86–91; and revolution 136, 138n7
shapeshifting 133n6, 137–138, 142
smoking 28–31, 39, 42, 110, 122, 132; *see also* witches
Stengers, Isabelle: *see also* otherworldly correspondence/imaginative leap; *see also* infernal alternative; and interstices 125–126, 135; and magic 121, 123–124, 126, 127, 139; and Science 77, 79–80, 81, 109–111; and thinking by the milieu 117; and thinking with Whitehead 104–107
surrealism 132–134; *see also* Césaire, Suzanne
surveillance 8–9, 11; of blackness 32–33, 91–92; of Muslims 2, 84–85, 92; *see also* prodrome; *see also* schools
suspicion 11, 49, 86–87, 91–93

terror: and American exceptionalism 20–21, 31–32, 89–90; *see also* art/public; *see also* coloniality; *see also* neocolonial security state; *see also* surveillance; *see also* suspicion; *see also* Tohunga Suppression Act; war on 2–3, 23–24, 27–28, 29, 34–35, 45–46; *see also* white supremacy
Tohunga Suppression Act 7–8, 118, 134
Trinh, Minh-ha 79–80, 82, 109–110, 122

whales 16, 28, 97–98, 112; *see also* border/breaching the; *see also* episteme/breaching the
white supremacy: and Dylann Roof 17–23; pillars of 2, 84–85, 91; and white fragility 80–85, 136–137; and white ignorance 1, 4–5, 9, 79–85, 98–99, 126, 136–137; and white women 6–7; and whiteness 3–6
witches 6–7, 42, 78–79, 110, 122, 124
worms 119–127
Wynter, Sylvia 7–8, 78–80, 109, 115–116, 135

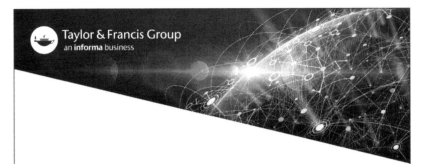

Taylor & Francis eBooks

www.taylorfrancis.com

A single destination for eBooks from Taylor & Francis with increased functionality and an improved user experience to meet the needs of our customers.

90,000+ eBooks of award-winning academic content in Humanities, Social Science, Science, Technology, Engineering, and Medical written by a global network of editors and authors.

TAYLOR & FRANCIS EBOOKS OFFERS:

- A streamlined experience for our library customers
- A single point of discovery for all of our eBook content
- Improved search and discovery of content at both book and chapter level

REQUEST A FREE TRIAL
support@taylorfrancis.com